Invisible Supp
Delivering the Differe... Curriculum.

by Jean Jameson

Barbara Maines and George Robinson,

Copyright Lucky Duck Publishing 1995
3 Thorndale Mews, Clifton, Bristol BS8 2HX
Tel: 0117 973 2881 Fax: 0117 973 1707
e-mail publishing@luckyduck.co.uk
Web: www.lukcyduck.co.uk

Second Edition 1998

ISBN 1 873942 90 7

Contributions, filmed and written, from

Portishead Primary School: a year two class with Angela Hawthorn,

Callicroft Junior School: a year six class with Steve Stickings,

Nailsea Comprehensive School: several subject lessons with David Pearce.

The video is introduced by Jean Gross.

A collection of support strategies, Appendix 3, was compiled by
Mike Connor, Surrey Educational Psychology Service.

The D.A.R.T.s activity, Appendix 4, is a contribution from
Margaret Byram, Avon Service for Special Educational Needs.

> We hope that the manual and video will generally be used together.

ISBN 1 873 942 90 7

Published by Lucky Duck Publishing Ltd
3 Thorndale Mews, Clifton, Bristol, BS8 2HX, UK

www.luckyduck.co.uk

Commissioning Editor: George Robinson
Illustrator: Mike Vening

Printed by Antony Rowe

Third reprinting, August 2003

© Jean Jameson, Barbara Maines, George Robinson 1995

All rights reserved. No part of this publication may be reproduced, stored in a retrieval system, or transmitted in any form, or by any means, electronic, mechanical, photocopying, recording or otherwise, without the prior, written permission of the publisher.

The right of the Authors to be identified as Author of this work has been asserted by them in accordance with the Copyright, Design and Patents Act, 1988.

Introduction

The Video

The video runs in a continuous sequence for thirty minutes. It was filmed in three schools and in it you will see a range of different support systems delivered by Angela, Steve and David. We do not claim that these are all new and innovative - much of it will be familiar and many primary teachers will watch the secondary footage and recognise their own classroom arrangements. We have collected examples of existing good practice and ideas as models. If you learn something or find a new idea then that is good. If you are doing it already, that is good too!

About half the filming is set in the secondary school because in that environment it was easy to find a wide range of different practice in one school. If you find yourself watching a strategy that you like or an intervention that you consider helpful, then please don't be put off because the filmed sequence was made with an age group very different to the one you teach. All the ideas can be adapted.

Because we set out to illustrate an "invisible" process the sequences are not dramatic. The captions and commentary provide the brief teaching points. These are discussed in more detail in the manual.

The Manual

The manual is divided into 7 sections, each is separately numbered

Introduction		**Pages 1 - 4**
Main Text	Jean Jameson has written the text and embedded in it are the three accounts written by the teachers featured in the video.	**Pages 1 - 27**
Appendix 1	Inset Activities	**Pages 1 - 12**
Appendix 2	Co-operative Games	**Pages 1 - 10**
Appendix 3	Support Strategies	**Pages 1 - 36**
Appendix 4	D.A.R.T.s example	**Pages 1 - 10**
Appendix 5	Bibliography	**Pages 1 - 3**

Brett's Story

My first knowledge of Brett goes back to when he was eight years old in a second year class of a mainstream primary school. Brett had been identified as a child with reading delay and was receiving extra help in a small group twice a week. The visiting teacher had been concentrating on a spelling programme and was delighted when the four boys in the group arrived breathless after play time shouting, *"Miss, Miss, we have been spelling!"* Thinking that her teaching was really effective she enthusiastically asked them to tell her what they had been spelling. *"We've been making witches spells, Miss."* they replied.

Only slightly disappointed she entered into their game and asked them how they would use their magic wands to cast spells on her. *"I would turn you into a wriggly worm!" "I would turn you into a creepy crawly spider!" "I would turn you into a slimy snake!"* they replied one by one. At this point Brett turned and looked up at her with big eyes and said, *"I would turn you into a pretty lady, Miss!"*

Brett's essential good nature combined with an unerring ability to say or do the wrong thing was already evident and continued to demonstrate itself at frequent intervals in both school and home settings. As he progressed through the school system he continued to receive extra teaching and he did make some measurable progress but not sufficient to allow him to function easily and successfully within the classroom. Brett's parents wanted him to do well and offered support and encouragement but this was construed by Brett as additional pressure. His difficulties increased when he transferred to secondary school and a series of minor misunderstandings accumulated into more serious misdemeanours.

I first met Brett at the beginning of his year 9 at a comprehensive school following his return to school after a week's head teacher's suspension for swearing at a teacher. Following an accumulation of a number of reports of provocative and "nuisance" behaviour he had sworn at a teacher and this was considered sufficiently serious to warrant removal from the school for a short time and referral to the educational psychologist.

I saw Brett on his first morning back in school and we had the following discussion:

BM:	*How do you feel about what happened?*
Brett:	*Well, I'm partly sorry Miss and I'm partly not sorry.*
BM:	*Tell me about the bit that is sorry.*
Brett:	*She's a nice teacher and I shouldn't have said what I did. It was wrong.*
BM:	*And what about the bit that is not sorry?*
Brett:	*I'm fed up with having extra help. I've had extra help for eight years and I still can't read. If I want to read a word I'll ask and if I want to spell a word I'll ask but I don't want any more extra help.*

At this point Brett's anger dissolved and he burst into tears and explained that he had been withdrawn from German for remedial English lessons. At first he had not minded but next week the group was going on a trip to Germany and Brett was excluded because he had not studied the language. This, as far as he could see, was his only chance to go abroad.

During the years of support teaching Brett had, of course, made progress but that was not how he saw it. With the very best intentions we had provided this boy with a sense of failure which had resulted in deteriorating behaviour and relationships within school. At the end of the fourth year Brett was excluded from school and placed in alternative special provision.

That meeting with Brett helped me to find a new set of values for the work that I wanted to do with young people, their teachers and carers. Above all I wanted to ensure that nothing I did would be damaging to self-esteem.

Invisible Support

The first working title for this document was "By Pass Surgery". Like so many working titles it was quickly dropped, not least because we feared that it might be mainly purchased by third year medical students and ignored by teachers. The concept we had in mind concerned "access to the curriculum for pupils with special educational needs". It is a phrase we read in almost every statement and in every school policy document on special needs in mainstream schools. The problem is that when the needs have arisen because of a learning or a behavioural difficulty then the teaching and the remediation processes may get mixed up, to the detriment of both. This is not so when the needs are, say, physical or sensory.

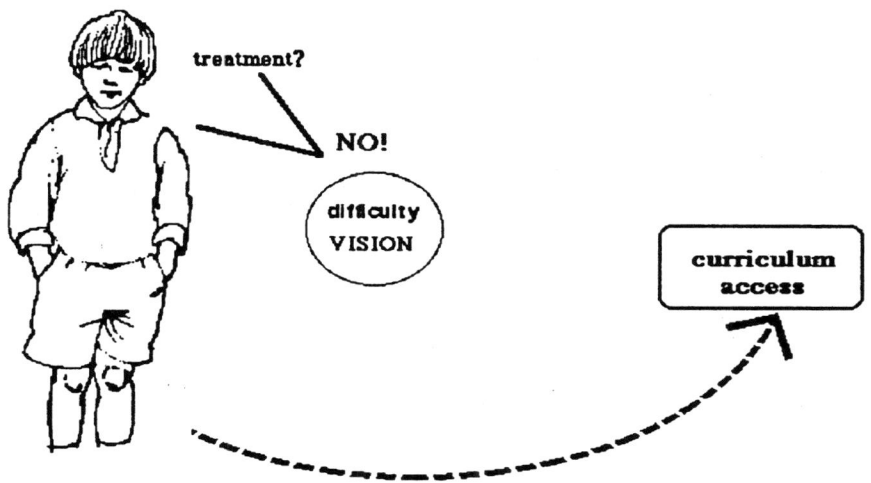

When a student appears in a classroom with a visual impairment the teacher does not urge her to look harder, try and see, have a go. The young person in a wheel chair is not asked to make an effort to walk. The access to the curriculum is ensured by bypassing the disability. Quite separately, and outside the classroom, the young person might be offered laser surgery or physiotherapy. If the disability is lessened, then the support structures can be modified or removed altogether.

When the barrier to access is reading or writing then the issues may become blurred. Content may be presented in text and responses required by writing. This provides continuous practice for the acquisition of the skills involved. In some cases this may bring about improvement. In many it will be nothing more than a practice of failure and a barrier to the curriculum access. For these children we have tried to treat their skills deficit in the same way that we would manage a sensory or physical impairment and separate the treatment programme from the structures planned to ensure curriculum access.

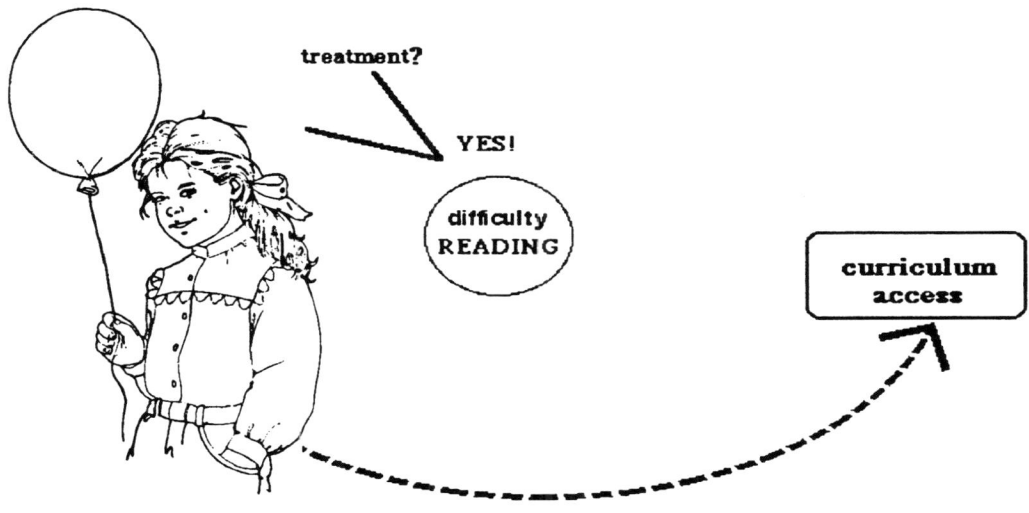

Introduction page 3

For the young people whose emotional and behavioural difficulties are the impediment to curriculum access, the support structures have been set into a whole class programme to build self-esteem and develop trust and co-operation which is carried on into the teaching and learning environment. In this way the young people can be helped in two ways:
  * the curriculum access is enhanced by "by-passing" their difficulties
  * the supportive learning environment improves relationships and reduces behavioural and emotional difficulties.

As the students achieve success there is a positive effect on self-esteem which in turn reduces the behavioural difficulties and improves the curriculum access.

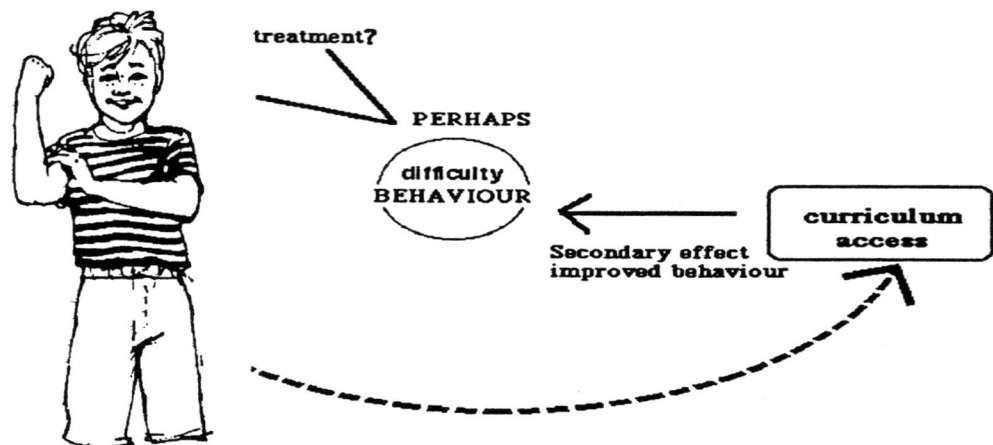

We have worked with many wonderful teachers and we couldn't film them all. The colleagues you see in this video were filmed in real classrooms working with their own students. Sometimes the young person modelling a learning or behavioural difficulty is "acting" for that particular demonstration. This was arranged to protect the self-esteem of their peers.

The hope is that this piece of work will add some ideas and strategies to the repertoire of all teachers who want to ensure that none of their pupils go through the education system feeling as Brett did.

Barbara Maines

Differentiation and Self-esteem in Ordinary Classrooms

Main Text   Jean Jameson has written the text and embedded in it are the three accounts written by the teachers featured in the video.

Pages 1 - 27

Differentiation and Self-esteem in Ordinary Classrooms

Introduction

"It has been long-standing government policy, confirmed in numerous official documents, that no child should be sent to a special school who can be satisfactorily educated in an ordinary one." (7.2, Warnock Report, 1978)

As part of the job, we are frequently reassessing what are the special educational needs of the young people we teach and how we can be sure to meet those needs "satisfactorily" in the context in which we are working. Shifting social attitudes to disability and inequality have influenced policy and practice in special education (Moon, 1990). Legislation for equal opportunities reflects a growing appreciation of the damaging effect of labelling and makes segregation of minority groups less socially acceptable.

One result of the changes in educational policy and practice over the last ten years is that fewer children are educated away from their peers in segregated schools, special classes or "bottom" streams. Maths and modern foreign languages are often the only subject areas where pupils in secondary education are put into ability sets. Elsewhere, they are taught in mixed ability groups, with a variety of teaching and learning styles.

In the Warnock Report (DES, 1978) the principle of integrating into mainstream schools as many children as possible, was based on the following premise:

"The purpose of education for all children is the same: the goals are the same. But the help that individual children need in progressing towards them will be different. Whereas for some the road they have to travel towards the goal is smooth and easy, for others it is fraught with obstacles." (page 5, Chapter 1)

This was carried forward in subsequent legislation:

- 1981 Circular 8/81: Education Act 1981. The 1981 Act stressed that special educational needs are relative and come from the interaction between the child and his or her environment.
- 1987 Special Educational Needs: Implementation of the Education Act 1981 (House of Commons Education, Science and Arts Committee, 1987)
- 1988 Education Reform Act
- 1993 Education Act. Included in part three of this act was a promise to establish a code of practice which " must be 'regarded' when making decisions." (Visser, 1993) This has turned out to be the most detailed and far-reaching guidance ever issued on this subject.
- 1994 Code of Practice on the Identification and Assessment of Special Educational Needs.

In the foreword and introduction to the Code of Practice (1994), the fundamental principles are described:

"that pupils with special educational needs require access to a broad and balanced education, including the National Curriculum and that the needs of most pupils will be met in the mainstream classroom, alongside their peers. " (page 2)

Because there is now an acknowledgement that labelling or categorising people according to learning difficulty or disability is, in itself, disabling, there are fewer schools with rigidly defined special needs units. In many schools, the name given to the special needs class often becomes a derogatory name throughout the school. The remedial class students incur taunts of "remmies" and the Individual Group Study pupils became the "igs-pigs", even to the staff who teach them. In one school, the Learning Support Department changed its name from Special Needs more than five years ago, but the old name is still sometimes used, by staff and pupils, usually in an uncomplimentary context.

There is a link between labelling and allocation of resources as discussed in Pumphrey and Reason (1991) and it would be politically naive not to bear those considerations in mind when deciding on systems and procedures of support. In Avon, resources for statements of educational need are allocated on a matrix and based on individual education plans for pupils. This allows each school to make decisions about the nature of support needed in order to deliver an appropriately differentiated curriculum.

Differentiation: Why, What and How?

Why?

The "Why" is the easiest question, answered already by some of the previous discussion. If pupils of different abilities are going to learn together, then they will need different tasks, styles of teaching and resources to match their differing learning needs. (Ainscow, 1991, Visser, 1993, Spillman, 1991)

There has always been differentiation by outcome and the GCSE examination papers are a good example. Within the broad tiers, students are given the same tasks and then publicly graded according to their response, or "outcome". In the past differentiation meant a different curriculum, delivered in another setting, according to the perceived category of special educational need. (Pollard and Tann, 1987). Inclusive education brings differentiation into the mainstream classroom and relates it to a continuum of individual needs. King (1990) suggests it is about,

> "Developing expertise in differentiating by task and outcome and addressing all the implications these have for teaching styles and classroom organisation."

In primary schools differentiation is more widely accepted and practised than in secondary schools where the move away from setting is slower and the predominant teaching style is didactic. Differentiation is more than giving out worksheets in different colours for students to work through, all at the same time. Differentiation means a change in this static, traditional classroom. It means groups of students talking together, individuals proceeding at their own pace, a range of activities and resources available to students at different times and the teacher meeting needs as they arise around the teaching room. Primary teachers often work like this. Some secondary teachers have been resistant to such an approach, partly because they feel restricted by the pressure of an examination curriculum and partly because there are discipline implications. It is more challenging to keep control of an informal session than one where the students are safely strapped into their seats by the monologue from the front!

What?

The second question is "what" is differentiation? The OFSTED Handbook for the Inspection of Schools, (1993 H.M.S.O.) has a summary with key questions that should be asked including,

> "Does the school promote the education of all its pupils and provide a learning environment which supports individual academic, social and personal development?"

Differentiation is mentioned throughout the handbook in relation to all subject areas and not restricted to special needs.

In the new booklets describing the National Curriculum, the need for differentiation is recognised and defined:

> "For the small number of pupils who may need the provision, material may be selected from earlier or later key stages where this is necessary to enable individual pupils to progress and demonstrate achievement. Such material should be presented in context suitable to the pupil's age." (English in the National Curriculum, HMSO, 1995, page 1.)

Here are a few definitions of differentiation:

> "the means by which we help ALL pupils to be EFFECTIVE learners with CONTROL over their own learning." (Jeffs, 1991)

"curriculum objectives, teaching methods, assessment methods, resources and learning activities are planned to cater for the needs of individual pupils." (NCC, 1991)

"It is in part a matter of technique but also centrally a complex matter of finding conceptual, evaluative and practical ways of resolving tensions between important and basic human values." (Norwich, 1990)

"The matching of work to the abilities of individual children, so that they are stretched, but still achieve success." (NCC, 1993)

"It involves matching teaching and learning styles to enable pupils to progress through a curriculum." (Visser, 1993)

How?

The "How" question is the really chunky one. This package attempts to peel back the onion skins and identify the existing classroom activities which can be recognised as putting into practice the definitions given above. By matching the right activities or resources to the needs of the learners, teachers will be giving invisible support to those students.

Implications for differentiation in a mainstream classroom:

There needs to be:

- equality of opportunity
- clarity of purpose
- clarity of outcome
- aims must be achievable
- knowledge of the student
- a variety of tasks, open ended, to allow all students to complete task, or closed, with different tasks for different students or stages for students to work through
- a possibility for individual aims in skills development (language, or IT)
- a variety of resources
- displays of key words, information or task clues
- appropriate arrangement of furniture to match style of working
- clear expectations of student and teacher
- negotiated success criteria
- clear instructions
- time to review
- an atmosphere of collaboration and co-operation
- flexibility
- trust
- sufficient support to facilitate success

(Adapted from Angela Hawthorn, 1994, unpublished paper.)

In "Guidelines for Staff", (1991) Alvin Jeffs summarises the important role to be played by support teachers in his discussion of differentiation:

"If support teachers are to be really effective in providing a properly differentiated curriculum for pupils with learning difficulties, they must make significant contributions to a number of aspects of classroom organisation."

Support Within the Classroom as the Way Forward?

Supporting children of all ages in the ordinary classroom, alongside their peers, is not an easy or complete alternative to segregation. The phrase "in-class support" is used to describe various situations across the age range of formal education, where, for a variety of reasons, another adult works in a mainstream classroom alongside the teacher. For a child with a physical disability or a sensory impairment, "in-class support" can mean an adult in the classroom whose only function is to work with that one child. The success of this support depends not only upon the needs of the student and the skills of the supporter but also upon the relationships between all of those involved and their opportunity to negotiate a system that will work. Liaison about lesson aims and methods of working is essential if the possibilities of the situation are to be maximised.

One such classroom assistant in Somerset, Bill, found himself in the difficult position of wanting to move away from his charge as the boy grew in independence. However, the classroom teacher viewed the changing roles with suspicion. Bill's success at reading stories, playing the guitar and engaging the attention of other difficult pupils was seen as a threat to the authority of the regular class teacher. Other children were discouraged from going to Bill for help. The statemented pupil was thwarted in his bid to be more independent and the classroom assistant felt frustrated and under-used.

The Background

Infant classrooms have traditionally welcomed the presence of other adults, often a team of nursery nurses and volunteers work together. The emphasis here is often on sharing the physical care of the children and working together on social skills, with the teacher coordinating education programmes for each child. An article in the TES, January 27th 1995, describes one county's training scheme, funded by the DfE in twenty-seven centres around the country, for Specialist Teacher Assistants. The course organiser, John Bald, is quoted as saying it will provide *"an extra mind in the classroom, not just a pair of hands"*.

Junior schools, too, are used to working with other adults, either in team teaching situations where different areas of the curriculum are delivered by colleagues working together, with support assistants or teachers supporting specific children and volunteer parents listening to children read, helping with cooking, swimming or cycling proficiency.

It has been a very different scene in most secondary schools. There have been some experiments with team teaching, particularly in the days before the National Curriculum. Henbury School, in Bristol, for example, experimented with delivering history through lead lessons to a whole year group together in the hall with follow up work in classroom units, written and presented by a team of teachers. In general, secondary lessons have been taught in closed classrooms by the designated member of staff to the same group of pupils for at least one academic year.

When teachers in training take over a class it is usual for the teacher to withdraw to a polite distance. The opportunity for an experienced teacher to teach alongside a student or an NQT is not often taken up. Appraisal and action research techniques involving lesson observation and "critical friends" may not be welcomed (Hopkins, 1985). Help from parents or volunteers has usually been restricted to out of classroom activities, such as library work and help with sports teams or school trips.

Some subject teachers might well prefer to keep the class to themselves with the "difficult to teach" pupil taken out of the class and given appropriate help elsewhere. At this stage, the pupil with learning difficulties has often also become "difficult" in terms of disruptive behaviour and a range of well developed defensive strategies.

When young people transfer to a secondary school they will meet many different subject teachers, all with different methods and styles, and responsible for the delivery of only a part of the curriculum. If a pupil is to be offered support teaching it is more likely that this will be targeted on particular subjects or for the acquisition of identified skills. The help has generally been delivered to the child by withdrawing her from the classroom setting individually or in a small group, or by the segregation of a group of slower learning pupils into a "bottom set".

The complexity of the subject timetable and the shortage of planning time has served as an encouragement to maintain these models, especially as they do provide evidence that the support is actually delivered to the intended pupils. For a young person with a statement of special educational need there will be a requirement to account for the extra support or teaching time funded by the LEA. The system of tiers of GCSE papers is an added pressure to sort students accordingly into sets or bands. At a time when the effectiveness of mixed ability teaching is being questioned, it is even more important for learning support managers to marshal the evidence to best meet the needs of those vulnerable pupils they seek to support.

Is it a Question of " Either / Or"?

Some, especially older pupils, can be disturbed by either withdrawal or in-class support if the help serves to reinforce feelings of inadequacy. A support teacher who is always hovering just behind or beside a pupil with whom there is little relationship or rapport embarrasses the pupil by her presence. Putting a "parrot on the shoulder" support teacher in with a reluctant learner in year nine can exacerbate problems for the targeted pupil, the class teacher and the other pupils. There is a wonderful opportunity to play off one teacher against the other, undermining authority and classroom management, with the rest of the class as an audience.

> *Brian is fifteen and has had a statement since he was at junior school. He has not acquired the necessary literacy skills he needs to access the curriculum. He has made good progress over the last few years but will still need a reader and scribe in his GCSE history exam. He has learnt to "manage" his in-class support to suit his own needs whilst protecting his not inconsiderable "street cred" as captain of the school rugby team. He expects his support teacher to sit on the other side of the classroom, not acknowledge him in any way until the end of the lesson when he collects from her a set of simplified lesson notes and suggestions about how to tackle the homework. He can explain how embarrassing he used to find it to have his own teacher sitting by him and working with him in lessons. He also agrees that he would not like to have been taken out into a separate group.*

The dilemma is how to provide increasing autonomy for pupils without being seen doing it. It was this quest which led to the idea of "invisible support". It is difficult to describe to parents how their child's needs are being met when the support is no longer as "visible" (and therefore accountable) as when withdrawal classes were provided. We needed a phrase to describe the process we were striving for. Although references to strapless bras and surgical trusses were never made explicit, the idea of a collection of planned and anticipated activities, attitudes and resources packaged together to meet identified needs makes sense as "invisible support".

It is only the name which is new: there are many examples of good practice in supporting learners while preserving their dignity and self-esteem (Gilbert and Hart, 1990, Raban and Postlethwaite, 1988, Ainscow and Florek, 1989). We are trying to identify the constituent factors of that good practice and highlight the importance of recognising it.

Who Can Provide Invisible Support?

1. Teachers, with or without "specialist training", providing extra teaching for pupils with statements of educational need.

This time is used specifically to target pupils who have been identified as having significantly greater difficulty in learning than their peers. It is focused more and more often within the classroom and traditionally is the most "visible" form of support. When used for children with a physical need or sensory impairment, this kind of support is a direct link into the normal curriculum.

When used for pupils with general or specific learning difficulties, there may be a problem in that the support teacher feels that they are "cheating" the identified pupil if their attention is not directly focused on him or her. Parents who have battled for extra resources for their child may want to "see" evidence that the support is in place. A classroom teacher faced with a difficult pupil might also want attention focused on that child. However, in terms of building skills in independent learning, nurturing self-esteem and being able to anticipate and therefore remove difficulties before they arise, this situation cries out for the more distanced approach. This is illustrated in the video by David Pearce in several classroom activities in the secondary school.

2. General Assistants or Special Needs Assistants who are also supporting pupils with statements of special educational needs.

In all sectors of education, but more often in primary schools, adults are being paid on general assistant scales to meet some of the needs of statemented pupils. Hampshire County Council is one of twenty-seven counties to take part in a training scheme, offering a City and Guilds qualification, "Certificate in Learning Support". Glenys Fox (1988) has written a brilliant handbook for the course which succinctly describes the present situation, the context such assistants will be working in and some of the questions they should be asking. Fox quotes from the Audit Commission/HMI handbook:

> "Where extra help is provided, planning and communication are the keys to improving its impact."

The focus of authority and responsibility are different when the supporter is not also a teacher, but some of the questions raised are relevant to all support situations and we have included them in an INSET activity in Appendix 1. The following features of a support role are also relevant:

- promoting independence
- inspiring confidence and trust
- valuing the child
- fostering peer group acceptance
- encouraging and giving rewards
- developing listening skills
- enabling the child
- knowing the background
- finding out about the special need
- keeping confidences
- being "in tune" with the child's physical needs.

3. General Learning Support Teachers and "free" subject teachers

In primary and secondary schools support has often been provided by an extra teacher attached to a class to support those pupils who need help but do not have a statement. In some junior schools this is the way the head keeps her hand in. In some secondary schools teachers are freed from a proportion of timetable commitments and are able to work in their own specialist subject area. There is great potential here for developing differentiated, specialist resources which can then be used in subject lessons. If these teachers are also recognised as faculty representatives on the learning support team and have training sessions and regular meetings, there is a potential for a huge leap forward in the process of implementing a "whole school approach" to meet learning needs. A less satisfactory version of this system is when the "free" teachers have no choice about their deployment and are imported into colleagues' classrooms with little room for negotiation.

4. Volunteers: parents or sixth-formers

In this situation, the supporting adult is more likely to look to the classroom or subject teacher for guidance about their role in the classroom and it is easier for them to focus on meeting general needs as they arise around the class, including extension work for able pupils.

In the video Angela Hawthorn explains how she provides training for parents and other volunteers in her classroom and how important it is to use their help effectively. In the secondary school sixth-formers who volunteer to work in this way are given a course of training sessions which cover the importance of self-esteem, different learning strategies and the role they can play in facilitating learning.

5. Other Learners

We hope that the video illustrates an ethos of mutual support and tolerance of differences which helps to foster peer support in all three sectors. Later on in the section headed "Peer Support" the role of other pupils in the class is discussed further. In Steve's class, the social skills games underpin the delivery of a differentiated curriculum and in Angela's infant classroom, the pupils are encouraged to work in mixed ability groups, helping each other to contribute to the activity. In each of the secondary school scenes, pupils are sitting with friends and are encouraged to work together, discussing issues of content and process.

In many instances, practising teachers will recognise skills and techniques they have always used in their management of the ordinary classroom and in accommodating individual needs of pupils. We hope to illustrate and draw attention to a wide range of these skills and techniques in order to:

* reinforce and encourage existing good practice
* offer some new ideas
* provide material for training, supporting and encouraging inexperienced support people
* provide triggers for whole staff discussion on a school policy for support provision.

What you'll see in the video

In the video we visit three different school settings: an infant class, a junior class and a comprehensive school. In each one we have filmed good practice in supportive educational management. Within the restrictions of time the scope was limited and it was not possible to illustrate the full range of experience and expertise known to us. We hope the selection we made is of interest and adaptable to other settings not filmed.

We are very grateful to the teachers and their pupils for their patience and co-operation in sharing their experiences.

Throughout the film, there is an emphasis on creating a learning environment where everyone feels safe, where responses from teachers are positive and encouraging, where fear of failure is minimised and where motivation to make progress is maximised by the existence of a wide range of resources and strategies to support teaching and learning.

The Use of Volunteers and Resources in an Infant Classroom

In the infant classroom, Angela talks about how she tries to support all learning by maintaining a positive and tolerant atmosphere where the children can work in mixed ability groups, encouraged by each other. She provides a wide range of resources which help the children develop the cross-curricular skills needed for successful learning.

To integrate successfully all the different activities and resources Angela has in her classroom, it is vital to have other adults to help who understand what she is hoping to achieve. Her aim is to differentiate the way the children access the curriculum whilst enriching the learning experience for all her pupils. She explains how important it is to be clear about your expectations of adults who volunteer to help in the classroom.

> *"It is important at the outset to clarify your expectations and be explicit about the purpose of the session and exactly what encouragement to offer the children."*

Angela recognises the different strengths and interests of her volunteers and their preferences for certain activities. She builds on that and in her training sessions she gives specific examples of how to encourage and praise children.

> *"I find tremendous encouragement from hearing them talk so positively about the children, sharing with delight in their achievements."*

The Language Master and Breakthrough to Literacy

In the video, you see pupils working on the Language Master, recording and playing back their own voice, reading the sentences they have written and then extending that work by using their Breakthrough folders.

> *"Having to speak into a microphone encourages the children to plan what they want to say and express themselves in complete sentences. The sentences they have just created on the Language Master can be recreated on their word slide. This will involve them in word recognition, matching and sequencing and yet remove from them the physical manipulative skills required in writing until they have practised these skills in another context."*

The sentence strip can be scribed by an adult and covered in clear adhesive film, to be stored as a visual record of the pupil's work. (In Appendix 3 page 20 there is a reference to Colin Lane's work on A.R.R.O.W. and own voice recognition as an aid to learning.)

Brainstorming
At the beginning of a new topic or project Angela's pupils are encouraged to brainstorm, an activity usually reserved for in-service training! The basic principles, accepting each contribution without argument and presenting the overall result as a group effort, underlines the philosophy of valuing individuals and their efforts. It also provides another opportunity to write with different pens and present writing in a different format. The finished display of words and phrases provides reading material, a reference point for the ensuing work, a purpose built dictionary and a prompt for writing. It also introduces pupils to the idea of planning and organising their work. They are involved right from the beginning and that contribution makes them feel more "engaged" in the work that follows.

This is such a simple and free device and could easily be used with older pupils to advantage. In subjects such as science and humanities, opportunities to brainstorm points which should be covered, questions which should be asked and the order in which the work could be tackled would greatly increase the involvement of pupils in their own learning. "Ownership" of learning is important and has been made more difficult by the restrictions imposed by the National Curriculum. This strategy could allow some of that ownership.

Computers and Mixed Ability Co-operative Learning
Angela has a computer with a Concept keyboard attached to it. This is a touch sensitive pad which can be programmed to respond in many different ways to make access to the computer easier and more exciting. The concept keyboard can be covered with a choice of overlays of graded difficulty, sometimes made up from sentences created by the previous Language Master work, or a series of pictures as seen in the film. When pressed sentences appear on the screen and the story can be built up in the right order. The programme the pupils are using in this part of the film is Stylus Plus, which is a writing programme which will speak back what has been written. This helps them to correct their mistakes themselves as they listen to their story being read back.

The "invisible" component of this activity is the group co-operation. The activity is highly motivating and each child wants to take part. The mistakes are easily corrected and because the words seem somehow distanced and impersonal once displayed on the screen, no one child feels responsible for the errors, or embarrassed by personal failure. The group works together with determination, lots of communication and concentration and evident enjoyment.

Angela's Story

During the course of life there are events and people, particularly significant because of the impact they make on you. Martin was one of these people, only nine years old he had been in my class a matter of weeks when he presented me with a piece of writing which was going to change both of us. It was a sad and laboriously written piece of prose which began,

> *"I'm no good to anyone I can't do anything".*

I was in the middle of an INSET course at the time and decided that I would choose Martin as the subject for my child study. I knew that this would involve going into his home to observe him in his family setting while he carried out a variety of tasks. I had no idea at that point what opportunities this would open up for us both.

After several weeks and a number of visits my relationship with the family was such that I was able to ask his mother if she would like to come into the classroom. Although naturally a very shy person she agreed to come in and offer her help with craft activities. This opened the doors in a primary school which was fairly reticent about asking parents into the classroom. Before long a regular band of mums and dads came in once a week to support a number of craft and games activities. Martin meanwhile began to gain confidence. At the end of that year I left to work with the Special Educational Needs Support Service and Martin was a much happier and socially integrated boy.

Some years later I met Martin again, this time as a cashier in a large supermarket. He recognised me and smiled, I felt a warm glow of satisfaction to think that Martin had been able to achieve success and find steady employment. Then he added that he was just filling in time before starting university to read history. Duly chastised by my limited expectations for Martin, I determined that I would strive to offer all children the kind of support that would enable them to feel valued both as people and as learners.

The methods you see in the video are just some of the range of activities that I have introduced into the classroom. Although each activity is valid in itself because of the set of skills that are practised, they are there primarily because they increase the opportunities for all the children in the class to become successful, confident and happy learners.

Working with other adults

I have found it of tremendous value to have other adults supporting children in the classroom. The school general assistant has been assigned to my class for a little of the time but I have also been able to welcome parents into the classroom, as well as students, pupils on work experience and the assistant from the General Stores.

At the beginning of each year, parents are sent a letter listing the various areas in which support would be welcome. This includes classroom support, helping with school visits and administrative tasks such as book covering, typing and helping with the school library... something for all! Parents are asked to reply on the inevitable tear off slip and the information is collated and given to the appropriate teachers to organise. This has formed a good basic resource bank of helpers and offers some guidance to teachers looking for specific skills.

Before they arrive in school to help, new parent helpers are given written guidance which includes the domestic arrangements, where the tea and coffee are and which toilets to use, as well as a description of their role in the classroom as "encouragers and supporters". It also emphasises the importance of confidentiality. When parents are working within the classroom they may see and hear things which cause them to form opinions about children or teachers. It is vital that these are not discussed outside. It is also important that when they are working with groups of children they remain under the supervision of the teacher.

Language Master

One of our favourite pieces of equipment is the Language Master. Very popular a few years ago and often used for phonic practice, they seem to have spent a lot of time recently lingering in the back of stock cupboards. We use it often as part of the writing process. Adult support is particularly useful as children find it quite difficult at first to press the buttons and put the cards through at the critical moment. They soon become proficient at the mechanics but initial support avoids the feelings of failure which may accompany a number of false starts. It isn't long before all the children are able to produce several sentences using a number of cards each. They support one another in composing and editing the cards and encourage one another to make the sentences longer, an opportunity to develop the use of adjectives and adverbs. At times the activity can become quite intense as they attempt to get their pre-planned sentence onto the card length. I have seen usually unmotivated learners standing over the Language Master trying to get those last few words in before the tape runs out. The adult role is also to act as scribe. When the child is satisfied with the sentence it can be written on the card. I have covered all the blank cards with clear film and we use non-permanent pens.

Some children are able to scribe their sentences on their own cards after recording. Mistakes can easily be corrected. As the children become more confident, this becomes an independent activity. Sometimes, the machine and the cards become part of a display so that all children can read and listen to the writing of others. The cards are easily cleaned ready to use again.

Brainstorming

Alongside the activities seen on the video, a group of mixed ability children were making a large poster of words and phrases using an assortment of brightly coloured marker pens. The rules of brainstorming apply so that everybody's contribution is valued and questions and clarification are left until the feedback stage. Children are free to experiment with language and make their contribution to a group or even class activity, with the added treat - using the teacher's special pens!

The finished (often not a space to be found) sheet is an ideas poster generated by the children. It makes a valuable focus for discussion. The ideas can be clarified with an adult and small group together, and then shared with the whole class. Several children have become writers through the freedom that this activity gives them. They are not restricted by the conventions of writing books, sentence making, spelling or even holding a pencil correctly. They often choose to stand, reaching further into the middle of the poster to find space. The same phrase or word may appear several times in different colours or in different spellings.

In the Autumn, we cut out some of the words and pasted them on to a display of seasonal drawings. Our fireworks brainstorm was so vivid and dynamic that it became part of the display. Sometimes the brainstorm goes home with a child but it has always added to the class word resources. My use of "we" is significant because I feel that it is important that the outcome is negotiated, it is their brainstorm and belongs to the group.

Concept Keyboard

For many children the computer is a great motivator. With the addition of the touch sensitive board it becomes a particularly versatile and supportive piece of classroom equipment. The program the children use in the video has the added facility of a talkback. This enables them to check their work by hearing the computer read it to them. For the adult ear this can be quite a violation but for the child who is used to the electronic voice it only adds to the fun element of using the computer to do work. It also seems to encourage them to interact with the computer and each other as the video illustrates. If this activity is to work well the teacher will need to plan the make-up of the group with some care. In this case a lively confident child involves the others in the activity, but be aware that a dominant child can quickly change the nature of the activity into a passive spectator task for most of the group.

I have found this program particularly easy to use when I make my own overlays. I keep three frameworks stored so that I can type new information in with minimum effort. One can be used to make overlays that practise sequencing, reading, recall skills similar to the one that the group of children are using on the video to rewrite the story of Hansel and Gretel. This same framework was used on another occasion for a group of children to make an overlay for their friends to use. This time the children drew their own pictures to illustrate "The Story Of Milk" and stuck them on the rectangular frames. They decided what they wanted each frame to say and I typed in the words. An alternative format can take their words and phrases from the Language Master cards and from the brainstorming process to enable them to write using the overlay. Often I add little illustrations to support their words and phrases to make it easier for them to recognise and select them. In my experience some children move very quickly to the stage of wanting to supplement the overlay with extra words and they can do this quite simply by using the keyboard.

Parents are sometimes reluctant to support this activity because they have no experience of computer technology. A short teaching session boosts confidence and if things go wrong in a session there is usually at least one child who is able to put it right.

Word Folders

I have found that children respond enthusiastically to using these folders to support their writing. The words in the folders are gathered over a period of time and stored alphabetically. In this way dictionary skills are continually practised and reinforced as they return and retrieve words. Each folder also contains some blank cards. These can be inserted into sentences as children find the need for new words.

The adult role is again to support and encourage the children as they progress. The experienced adult can begin to judge when a child is ready for help or when a child just needs some adult encouragement to keep up the level of involvement. It is important to recognise when a child is thinking and actually does not require adult interference. The new adult in the classroom needs to be given guidance, particularly with the level of support required, the writing style to use on the cards and which children are more likely to need more immediate attention. Some children will expect the word to be written for them, while others will have a go at their own spelling. It is important that this is made explicit at the outset for the adult supporter, in negotiation with the child.

Tape Recorders

One of my parent helpers particularly enjoyed working with groups of children using the tape recorder. Over a period of time she developed ways of encouraging children to plan and present stories and descriptive passages. I found it was useful at first to listen together with the children to the tape, and then use it as a discussion point with the parent. The tape recorder can be used to develop ways of illustrating stories with sound effects, enables them to experiment with a range of voices and also encourages children to listen. I also record stories at home and have encouraged parents to do the same. The children enjoy the stories but also the fun in recognising whose parent is telling the story.

In the classroom at any one time, all or some of these activities may be taking place. This range of activities and resources can be used in a cross curricular way to record science, share information and express ideas. Tape recorders and Concept Keyboard overlays can provide another route for children to access information.

The introduction of the National Curriculum has made a number of increased demands on teachers and makes explicit the variety and range of skills that children should be developing. This list of skills and processes are taken from the programmes of study for the three core subjects of the National Curriculum.

Personal/ social skills:
   collaborating
   sharing
   discussing.
Cognitive skills:
   exploring and investigating
   raising questions
   forming and testing hypotheses
   interpreting results
   looking for and recognising pattern
   sorting and classifying
   planning and evaluation
   making choices and deciding drafting
   reflecting
   selecting equipment and materials
   checking and monitoring.
Communication skills:
   explaining
   reporting and describing
   discussion and debate
   recording and presenting
   listening/ reading/ writing
   using information.

Using a variety of equipment in the classroom is a way of providing a number of structured learning situations which will enable these skills to develop. Observing groups of children at work will show that while each resource makes different demands on the participants, adults will need to be aware of the purpose of the task, so that they can facilitate the learning process. This will ensure that children are given opportunities for discussion, collaborative working and also given the opportunities to make mistakes and be fully involved in reviewing and editing. One of the most important elements has been the enjoyment for the children who have developed and improved their writing skills. They approach tasks with increased enthusiasm and are able to express preferences for the resources they want to use.

The strength of Angela's approach is that all pupils, not just those who are finding learning difficult, will benefit from a wide range of multi-sensory learning opportunities when provided in an environment that encourages individual effort and achievement.

The Junior Classroom

Steve began to concentrate on finding "invisible" ways to change the learning environment in his classroom, after a particularly difficult time with a year six class. He realised that the children were not engaging with the content of the curriculum, partly because they were so uncomfortable working together and lacked the social skills to do so. He began to experiment with ways of by-passing the behaviour problems by differentiating the activities in the classroom and then tackling the other problems by introducing games to increase social integration and self-esteem.

He began by building on his knowledge and use of Teacher Effectiveness Training by Thomas Gordon (1974) and incorporating games to enhance positive child self-concept.

Steve's Story

Access to the Curriculum using Differentiation and Enhancing Pupil Self-concept

The School and Setting

The school was built during the 1960's, and consists of eight interconnecting classrooms on two floors around a quadrangle with one large hall. The building is set at the edge of a large grassed playing field and has one rectangular Tarmac playground with almost no play facilities. The catchment area is a large council estate intermixed with private houses. There are very few community facilities. At the time of writing there has been a rapidly rising level of unemployment as the main industrial employers cut their workforces. There are a large number of children with special educational needs, but the school is in an anomalous situation in that there is a comparatively small number of free school meals, the basis for extra funding in Avon. This means that the school budget allocation for special needs is relatively small. However, because there is a need for the support of SEN children, a sum of money has been set aside by the school to provide a permanent .4 support teacher. This person generally works with small withdrawal groups, but can work within classes if the teacher wishes. There is also G.A. help for each class for half a day per week.

Description of the Class

The class was made up of ten girls and twenty one boys. Sixteen were formally identified as having specific learning difficulties, two girls and fourteen boys. Five children were statemented, all boys: two for learning difficulties, two for learning, emotional and behavioural difficulties, and one academically very able boy for emotional and behavioural difficulties alone. The class had been taught the previous year as a split Yr 5/6 group by a very experienced teacher, who suffered a breakdown in her health which was directly attributed to the demands of the class as it was then constituted. She subsequently retired from teaching. At the time when the make up of the Yr6 class was being considered it was not known whether the teacher concerned would be returning to work, and because of organisational difficulties around staff and class numbers it meant that this teacher might have faced many of these children again as Yr6 pupils. For this reason the most challenging children were all placed in one class with a small number of children who had no major learning difficulties.

Since arriving in the school in Yr3, this group of children had been identified as being quite exceptionally challenging, even amongst a school population that was very demanding. As they moved through the school this reputation grew, with particular personalities standing out as very disruptive around the school generally. Indeed it is true to say that this group of children did have a very unusually marked effect on the way that many other children in the school conducted themselves and related to adults and each other. As the newly appointed deputy head I arrived and began to teach this class.

Is Remediation part of Differentiation?

When I met this group of children I very quickly became aware of a need for social skills and strategies for co-operation, but nothing prepared me for my first two weeks with them. Never before had I encountered a group of children like this, and never before had I encountered the feelings and emotions that I experienced, not even during teaching practice. I felt on the very edges of control, I experienced fear, deep and powerful frustration, and for me most shocking of all, intense feelings of anger which I didn't even know I had within me. On one day, the one and only day since I began teaching sixteen years ago, I actually said to myself: "I can't cope with this, I've lost my skills, I'm going to chuck it all in." I then had to fight to stay in the classroom until the end of the day, knowing that as the newly appointed deputy, all eyes were definitely pointed in my direction to see if I was going to sink or swim. I had reached a make or break situation. By the time I got home I had got over the "chuck it in" crisis, and spent that evening trying to identify what the key issues were that needed to be addressed, initially to contain the situation, and later to stand some chance of maybe turning it around.

I identified three crucial areas which needed to be worked on:

1) Almost all the children in the class had a very poor self-concept, for many different reasons, but being in a class labelled as a "problem" class affected them all. Individually I believed all the children were amenable and friendly, but collectively they seemed only able to relate to each other using verbal abuse, put downs, wind ups or physical intimidation. The use of any of these tactics briefly allowed the user to "be on top" and therefore to feel more in control. The need I identified was for ways of improving all the children's self-esteem, and providing a means to gaining social skills that would help them relate to each other more positively.

2) Any classroom activities had to be carefully differentiated so that the children were, and felt that they were, succeeding, regardless of their ability level. If they could feel good about their work, just maybe they might begin to feel better about themselves.

3) The school had introduced a policy of Assertive Discipline (an American behaviourist programme) at the start of the school year. It was clear that this group of children simply could not cope with the expectations of AD. If it was implemented as stated, then most of the class would be sent out of class or out of school every day. A modified approach had to be found which stayed broadly within school policy, but at the same time allowed the children to succeed in behaving more positively.

In all three problem areas a lack of social skills and low self-esteem are crucial impediments.

Possible Options

Addressing the poor social skills and low self-esteem of the young people

The curriculum is suspended and time is taken out to address the deficit directly. The aim of such an approach would be to return to teaching objectives once the necessary skills/level of self-esteem had been reached. This is an option which might have been possible before the introduction of the National Curriculum but without disapplying the NC from the whole class this would not now be acceptable.

Differentiation of learning tasks to ensure success and promote self-esteem

An attempt is made to "by-pass" the effects of the social skills and self-esteem deficit by producing learning activities which are differentiated and so intrinsically interesting and stimulating that the teaching objectives are achieved without addressing the deficit directly. I was not convinced that this would be possible without the work planned to address the deficit directly.

The combined effects of both interventions

A classroom programme which would provide strategies to improve self-esteem and social skills whilst the learning objectives were made safe by differentiation required very significant changes of the structure of the class but seemed to hold out the best hope for improvement and for maximisation of the combined effects of the two processes. Improved social skills and self-esteem would allow better curriculum access and educational success could improve social skills and self-esteem. One plus one might add up to three.

I felt the most effective way to improve social skills and self-esteem was by:
* The use of games designed to promote social skills, self esteem and co-operation.
* The extensive use of positive "I" language from the approach outlined by Thomas Gordon (1974).
* An extensive range of practical actions to give recognition for achievement and positive behaviour.

I felt the most effective way to by-pass the difficulty and allow curriculum access was by:
* The use of Directed Activities Related to Text, (D.A.R.T.) linked to a range of differentiated outcomes.
* A range of other approaches to differentiation.

I was then left with the third issue - the moderation of the school Assertive Discipline policy for this class of pupils. This might be achieved by:
* Drawing on the social skills work.
* Using active listening.
* Using the Three Part Confrontive "I" message.
* Modifying the method of warning children of an impending negative consequence.
* Making the steps towards a recorded negative consequence smaller but with more of them.
* Making regular contact with the parents of especially difficult children.

Addressing the Deficit Directly - Practical approaches to the promotion of enhanced Self-Concept and the development of Social Skills

Positive "I" statements are statements which are very specific, personal to the child concerned, and usually delivered informally on a 1:1 basis whilst working in the classroom. They follow this pattern:

"I really like your picture because the bright colours cheer me up."
"I am very pleased when you tidy up the room so carefully."

This discloses some of the teacher's personal feelings about the work and behaviour, identifies a specific quality, and avoids an empty value statement like "Good" or "Thank you". It only identifies positive qualities. This is easily illustrated with regard to the art work of children with low self-esteem. These children would frequently spoil their work deliberately, or throw it away, or start again calling it or themselves rubbish. By using a positive "I" message almost all of these children began to value their work and some actually seemed to physically "walk taller" with repeated requests to show their work to their previous teachers, the head or parents. This was clearly illustrated by a girl, Maria:

Maria was a less able child who found school work very hard and felt that she rarely achieved anything worthwhile. She often referred to herself and/or her work as rubbish. Her self-concept was very low. I first used the positive "I" message with a painting of a wet weather window. She wanted to throw it away. When I asked why she said, "Because it's rubbish - like me." I responded, "But Maria, you have made such a lovely mix of colours. They make me feel as though I am really looking through a wet weather window. If you do decide you don't want it please can I have it to take home." Maria's whole body language changed as I watched. She felt that she and her work were valued, (which they were) and she positively wanted to finish the painting, which she offered to me at the end of the term. This is one small example, but one which I was to see repeated many times.

Many of these children had little experience of receiving sustained positive messages about themselves. It therefore took some while before they were able to begin to accept what was being said to them, and in the case of Matt, one of the most disturbed children, it seemed as if positive "I" statements actually hurt in a physical way, to the point where I had to restrict the frequency for a short period. In the majority of children there was a definite response, but it seemed to me a very slow one. However, support teachers from outside the school (Support Service for Emotionally and Behaviourally Disturbed Children, and Service for Special Educational Needs) both stated that they were able to observe a marked increase in positive behaviours long before I was able to accept that something was happening.

Games to promote social skills and co-operation

In addition to the need for the use of positive "I" language, I had identified that as a group these children had very rarely had the chance to have fun as part of their learning activities. The main reason for this was that once control was relaxed even slightly, they tended to run amok. I needed to maintain my influence on the group and at the same time allow them to have fun, and therefore begin to relate co-operatively and positively with each other. I created a specific environment which was under my influence, but within which it was OK for them to become excited or boisterous. I obtained a parachute and began to use many of the parachute games designed to promote fun and maximise co-operation. Many of these are listed in: Meynell (1993), Olsen and Parker (1988), Heseltine (1987), Dewar, Palser and Notley (1989). See appendix 2 for short descriptions of the most used games.

In addition to this we began to regularly use games designed to promote social skills, and co-operation drawn largely from: Brandes and Phillips (1977), Wiltshire County Council (1991), Bliss and Tetley (1993), Caldecott, Durbin and Siner (1993).

I contacted:
* Bristol Mediation services for further training in promoting mediation between children.
* The Education Section of the Co-operative Movement to find out more about co-operative play.

The Co-operative Movement funded a one day co-operative play workshop for the whole school. This I followed up by setting up an after school club which rotated through year groups each half term, to consolidate a knowledge base of co-operative games which children could play without the supervision of adults.

The use of these games did start to have the effect I had hoped for, in particular the willingness to allow children to work nearer to each other's body zones, and a more positive sense of group identity. Probably the most important factor in these games is that they are a lot of fun, but in order to be fun, co-operation and close physical proximity to other children must be tolerated. The fun aspect is such a powerful medium of delivery that the co-operation and breaking down of body zones slips in and takes root incidentally and unnoticed.

Classroom recognitions for positive and appropriate actions

In the classroom I implemented an extensive range of recognitions for positive and appropriate actions. These can be divided into:

* Individual teacher recognitions.
* Whole class teacher recognitions.
* Individual child recognitions of other children.
* Individual recognitions by children of themselves.

Individual teacher recognitions included:

Stars on an individual card leading to a certificate. The child getting the highest number of certificates in a half term received a 1st and 2nd prize.
Praise notes home, design of note selected by individual child. Some notes previously designed by other children.
Special certificates for sustained and special effort for a period longer than one week.
A wide range of stickers and stamps used as badges.
Peas in a tube leading additionally to whole class recognition.
Black Jacks and Fruit Salads.
Telephone calls home to give positive recognition.

Whole class teacher recognitions
   Peas in a tube, as above, but tube used to recognise both individual and class as a group.
      Filled tube = five minutes extra break time.
   Five fillings of the pea tube = range of recognitions including:
   extra parachute time,
   free choice time,
   pop corn party,
   squash and biscuits,
   leisure video,
   picnic.
   Tally book, introduced specifically to support being able to settle to a task quickly and moving around the school as a group. Each tally mark was worth ten seconds of extra break time. Hand up for quiet and teacher counting slowly to three. Quiet by count of three = 1 tally, by two = 2 tallies, by one = 3 tallies.

Individual child recognitions of other children
All children's names placed on envelopes around edge of a pin board. Dress making pins stuck into pin board in middle area. In each envelope five card labels with the same child's name on and single hole punched. If John had done something positive for Emma, then Emma could go to John's envelope, take out a card with his name on it and display it by hooking it on the pins. This produced a map of children's names recognised by others for their positive actions. Who put the name up and why could then be discussed periodically at the end of the day or during circle times. This proved very popular and was not abused.

Individual recognitions by children of themselves
This involved having a supply of the same size card hexagons in a variety of colours and a supply of blue tack. Any child could take any hexagon and write on it her name, the date and anything that she had done in school which she felt good about. The hexagon then had to be placed next to any others which had been put up, so that it tessellated with those already in place. This resulted it a wandering beehive of good feelings that spread out in all directions around the room, the walls, ceiling, anywhere so long as it tessellated. Again this proved very popular and was not abused.

By-passing the deficit and accessing the curriculum using differentiated activities
It was clear that owing to the very high number of children having special learning needs, and the enormous span of abilities, I could not address specific special learning needs, this I felt was the most appropriate use of support teachers. I felt that the most effective and appropriate use of my time for learning and understanding was to provide access to the curriculum for all the children with activities which could also be drawn upon by the support teachers where appropriate. After long consultation with Margaret Byram, S.S.E.N. team leader for Northavon, it seemed likely that extensive use of D.A.R.T.s, linked to differentiated outcomes, would prove most effective and beneficial. I was already familiar with the principles and philosophy behind D.A.R.T.s as I had

already started to use them as part of the work I had begun around differentiation 18 months earlier. This meant I had an initial but not very developed base of knowledge and experience to draw upon. Selecting this approach also allowed me to make this a high enough priority to develop extensively my knowledge, practice and experience in this area. Using a "classical" approach to D.A.R.T.s also contained a very powerful element for working as a whole class, in a very simple and controlled way when reading chorally and focusing on a text together at the same time. Pairing able and less able children for this created new social groupings within a clear and positive framework, and when linked to follow up activities encouraged a high degree of co-operation. My use of D.A.R.T.s fell broadly into two categories, Reconstruction of text and Analysis of text (see appendix 4).

Although D.A.R.T.s formed the core of differentiated activities, it was by no means the only approach used, though it did often provide the stimulus for other approaches. For example, John and Alan coped well with their understanding of material on puberty and reproduction. They went on to make a series of Plasticine models showing in each case the womb and foetus at different stages, rather than making a written response. They went on to act as "consultants" in a Health Education display in school, where they explained their models. Other approaches used to allow access to the curriculum include:

> Paired reading - peer and adult.
> Varied grouping of children for different activities.
> Four step Cloze Procedure.
> Group Reading Activities.
> Oral Outcomes.
> Paintings / drawings.
> Posters.
> Another adult or child as Scribe.
> Sequencing.
> Taped outcomes.
> Taped reading materials, including maths scheme text book.
> Thesauruses.
> Use of alternate lines.
> Maths friend, (support by a previously identified peer).

Many of these approaches have been summarised in a very succinct and practical way in a booklet entitled Practical Approaches to Differentiation: A Handbook of Ideas for Teachers, Byram (1994).

Towards the middle of the Spring Term I was beginning to feel that as the children were able to access the curriculum through differentiated activities, and succeed academically in their own eyes, their levels of self-esteem were increased. The dual approaches were complementing each other. In order to test out my observations I again approached the Team Leader for North Avon SSEN, and asked her if she could spare the time to come and observe my class working. Her assessment was very significant in that it identified positive, crucial and significant changes in the children's working which were difficult for me to measure. These comments confirmed my hopes about the class, but in a much wider and far-reaching way than I had anticipated (see appendix four).

Drawing on the values that were emerging from the social skills and co-operation games, using active listening and "I" language, were all having an effect in promoting more positive behaviours. The issue of the school AD policy still needed to be addressed. The majority of children simply were not able to respond within the number of warnings and crosses advocated by Canter, regardless of whether a negative consequence followed. It seemed almost as if they heard the request or warning, but were unable to make the connection and respond as requested. After trying a number of different ways of resolving this I increased the number of steps before giving a negative consequence. This approach seemed to work much more effectively with the majority of the children and also allowed the use of the confrontive "I" language to head off both warnings and negative consequences. At the same time I targeted the seven or eight children who were not responding and conferenced with each child and parents to set up a system of incentives and disincentives to help support more appropriate and positive behaviours.

Reflections on the year as a whole

This was, without doubt, my toughest year in teaching, but for me confirmed beyond question the effectiveness of the two key strategies of enhancing child self-concept, and access to the curriculum through differentiated classroom activities. A year which had started with children who, instead of engaging with the curriculum, would sco-op up tadpoles into their mouths to use as pea shooters, or who would try to play rounders with potatoes in the classroom, or who would drive supply teachers away after only half a day, ended with a group of children who had made very definite steps forward both in their learning skills and their ability to relate to other children. Sadly much of the improvement in their relations with other children and adults was not transferred outside the classroom and around the rest of the school. Whilst I was able to change significantly the environment and expectations of the children within the classroom, I could not do this outside where the children were still locked into a pattern of largely negative behaviour. They were in fact trapped by five years of expectations from other children and adults, built upon self perpetuating negative behaviours. In the classroom those expectations had been suspended, giving them the freedom to take positive risks, and often succeed. Despite all my initial expectations I miss my little group of miscreant muppets!

The Secondary School Scene

David's role as a full-time support teacher in the learning support department of a large comprehensive school gave him the opportunity to try out several different models of support. Part of the department's development plan was to evaluate the effectiveness of in-class support and a survey of teachers' opinions was carried out.

One conclusion we came to very early on was that the model chosen has to be one with which both the support teacher and the subject teacher are comfortable. It is also not always possible to meet and liaise as often as necessary to work really well. The video shows the planning for one geography lesson "on the hoof" in the staffroom during the break before the lesson. Like marriages, some partnerships seem to work almost intuitively, others need greater negotiation and planning at the beginning and some need regular discussion and adjustment throughout.

Occasionally, the partnership doesn't work for all sorts of reasons, and has to be abandoned or re-negotiated. Sometimes the model chosen depends on the timetable and the amount of support time available. Real team teaching can only happen when the support teacher is time-tabled into all the lessons of that teaching slot, so planning, marking and teaching can all be shared equally. It is more often the case that the support teacher is only in one or two of the lessons the subject teacher has with that group and so part of the liaison time is catching up on what's happened in between. The class often sees the support teacher as not a "proper" teacher and there may be issues of authority and discipline.

David is seen in three different situations. Firstly, he is working in a geography lesson with Liz, where the class is shown how to draw climate graphs. They both know which pupils might find this difficult and once the task is set both teachers circulate, answering needs as they arise and encouraging pupils to take responsibility for their own progress. This is visible support, but the underlying strength of the support is the way both teachers listen to pupils who ask for help by going to them, not conducting the query publicly, and then crouching to their level and acknowledging the positive steps the pupil has already taken before addressing the problem.

In the second situation, David is seen team teaching with an English teacher, Sarah, in a year ten mixed ability English class. Lastly David works on differentiated resources to support pupils in a classroom where he is only an occasional visitor.

David, a support teacher in a secondary school

As teachers, how often do we ask pupils to share their work? Some are always willing to push themselves forward while others always hang back. I'm one of the reticent ones and it's only due to

Barbara's great powers of persuasion that I've taken part in making the video and I now find myself writing for the accompanying folder. My reticence comes from a fear that everyone's going to say, *"We do that anyway!"* I know that primary colleagues particularly will see the differentiation techniques as common place. Even so I hope all teachers will find some valuable ideas in my bits about how to establish successful teaching partnerships and support pupils in mainstream classes for I know that it's within these partnerships that I have done my most effective teaching. What I've written here falls into two main parts:
1. Developing Teaching Partnerships
2. The Value of In Class Support.

1. Developing Teaching Partnerships

There's no doubt that developing a teaching partnership takes time and commitment. Like wooing a lover, one has to be patient and tactful at first and even when we've been going steady I know that teachers have hidden in cupboards when they've seen me coming for another planning meeting! Even so, teachers working with the same class must have regular meetings and you mustn't be put off by teachers who say, *" Love to meet but sorry I haven't got the time."* Meetings don't have to be long and drawn out. I have a Rule of Meetings: if you've got an hour sit down and put the kettle on, if you've got less time sit down but don't make coffee and if you want it to be short don't sit down and don't drink.

The pressure of time is no reason for not sorting out teaching strategies before a lesson. Planning can be done effectively on the hoof as, for example, by me and Liz on the video in the staff room at break. We only needed a couple of minutes because we both knew the materials, the pupils and the respective roles we would take in the classroom.

However, there is also a need for longer meetings, particularly at the beginning of a topic. For example, the meeting to plan the approach to teaching map work skills that you see Clive and me having on the video lasted an hour. Most meetings aren't nearly that long because we have found ways of making them as short and efficient as possible:

1. Agree to meet at the same time in the same place each week
2. Apply the Rule of Meetings
3. Quickly agree who is going to do what work
4. Fix a time to meet again to show each other the work prepared.

In this way most of the work is done by teachers on their own and as teachers get more used to working with each other meetings get shorter. In a full team teaching situation like the Year 10 English lessons on the video, where Sarah and I were together for almost all the group's lessons, I've found it possible, once a topic has been launched, to do a lot of planning in the classroom as pupils are working. Clearly, support teachers must settle on an acceptable work load; some partnerships will involve more work and therefore more meetings but others can run effectively on a couple of minutes' consultation a week.

And that consultation is vital. However brief it's not just good to talk, it's essential. I am constantly surprised and delighted when a germ of an idea explodes into brilliance when I'm working with another teacher. And then there are two pairs of hands to put the idea into practice. I wonder how often teachers' good ideas come to nothing because they don't have the time to produce the materials. In teaching partnerships the single teacher's cry, "*If only I could!*" becomes "*Well, we can!*" Then the pack of resources and new strategies can be used by teachers working on their own. The map skills work and the work on Reicker shown on the video are two examples of this process at work.

My partnerships with Clive and Sarah that produced this work were particularly fruitful because I was working with established teachers who were interested in exploring new teaching approaches and who had a similar teaching style to me. Partnerships like this are not always possible or, indeed, appropriate. In the first place, no support teacher has the time or energy to work in this way all the time. Also, it is very important for support teachers to blend with the teaching style of the subject teacher. For example, the video shows me working with Liz and a Year 8 Geography class. Liz was in her first year of teaching, developing her own style, and so I decided it was best to let her do the main lesson planning and for me to concentrate on producing a few supplementary materials and supporting a few individuals in the class. This approach is also appropriate where a teacher is teaching a well known topic with plenty of good resources.

Whatever type of partnership teachers are involved in, I think it's very important for them to think through the roles they are going to play. Even if I'm only working with a class for one lesson a week, I like to establish myself by leading some lessons, setting homework and running class discussions. I think this helps the class to take the support teacher seriously and, more important, it allows the subject teacher to observe the class and to work closely with individuals without having to worry about what the rest of the class is doing. I know other support teachers don't agree and prefer to develop their role as the confidant and helper. Often pupils will identify their support teachers to me as the nice ones and I remember when I first began support teaching how a boy poured out his heart to me about his learning difficulties and how he wasn't going to do this stupid homework. He only told me all this, he said, because I wasn't a real teacher. No one way is the right way and it's important for teachers to agree on roles with which they are both comfortable.

2 The Value of In Class Support

During my time at Nailsea School I worked with the SENCO, Jean Jameson, and the rest of the Learning Support Department, to develop a system of in class support. Our aim was to integrate all pupils with learning difficulties into mainstream classes and support them there. We eventually coined the term invisible support to describe the system. In one sense, of course, the support was very visible. We put support teachers with a paraphernalia of equipment including laptops, tape recorders and video cameras, into classrooms. In another sense though our support was invisible. We aimed to create a climate in the classroom in which:

- Everyone knew they were equally important and had equally valuable contributions to make.
- Everyone accepted that they needed help at some time and that everyone was entitled to help.
- Co-operation and not competition was important and everyone would work with and support everyone else.
- There were a variety of ways of learning.

So, if pupils with learning difficulties were being helped by a teacher or were learning in a different way, they didn't stand out because that was the normal way of doing things. Their support was there and real but it was in effect invisible.

We set up this system because we were dissatisfied with other ways of teaching children with learning difficulties. Having taught in a school with streamed classes and Remedial / Special Needs / sink groups, I can write with feeling about how difficult these groups are to teach and how damaging they are to the pupils in them. Stigmatised as "remmers", pupils have a poor image of themselves as learners and low expectations of what they can achieve. The mixture of a wide range of often serious learning difficulties and behavioural problems makes class teaching difficult and the close individual help that pupils need almost impossible. There are few good working habits to copy and the main thing that many pupils learn is new ways to avoid learning.

Small group withdrawal from some lessons avoids some of these problems, but pupils are missing part of the curriculum. There is plenty of evidence to show that the skills learnt in small withdrawn groups are not transferred into other situations and, once again, pupils are separated from their peers and seen as different. This does little for their positive self-image and they are likely to see themselves as failures.

A successful system of in class support can be very different. Pupils with learning difficulties have access to the whole curriculum and work alongside their peers. They have hard-working role models to follow and with two teachers in one group it's easier for them to get the individual help they need. They are more likely to feel good about themselves and to achieve. Many of the responses to the questionnaire we sent to teachers backed up this positive picture of in class support. They noted how support teachers helped to improve pupil behaviour and generally encouraged a better working atmosphere.

It is also clear that in class support doesn't just benefit pupils with learning difficulties. It enables the children in the middle, who don't have serious difficulties, to get the little bit of help they need with their spelling or having something explained again in another way. My experience at Nailsea also lays to rest forever the old chestnut of children with learning difficulties in mixed ability classes holding back bright pupils. As Sarah says on the video about our Year 10 English work, *"It was as challenging as anything I've ever done before .... we put so much thought into the materials that they really stretched the kids as much as possible."* Nicola, a potential A grade candidate agrees. *"It's good because with two different ways of teaching something we have two different ideas. It inspires us more."*

The key to making all this happen is differentiation. The video shows two examples of differentiated topics from Nailsea School and I hope these illustrate the general principles involved. By differentiation I mean that pupils are offered a variety of learning opportunities, so that they can approach their work at their own level, in their own way and at their own pace.

In the map skills work, for example, pupils show what they can do through a simple self assessment and ask for help or testing as they need it.

Rather than sit with a hand in the air they record their requests for attention on the board.

This can produce surprises. As I say on the video, there's a lad, Jason, in this class who has severe reading and writing difficulties and we would probably have suggested that he started with the basic skills, but he knew what he could do and he could prove it. This setup also enables very able pupils to work at a level appropriate to them. On the video we see Michael undertaking the challenge of planning a walk for a person with a heart condition. Similarly, in the Reicker work we provided work at different levels. For example, pupils could choose to tackle the task of writing a story summary entirely on their own, with some helpful hints from teacher, or by sequencing some cut-up sentences. We also organised some group work at different levels. We arranged groups by ability and then set them tasks appropriately, ranging from a character study of Reicker to analysing the use the author makes of setting to underpin the themes of the story. Each group had to present its work, thereby valuing each contribution equally.

Just as important as setting work at different levels is encouraging pupils to work in a variety of ways, so that they can use their preferred learning styles. For example, on the video we see two Year 10 pupils opting to listen to a story on tape rather than read it. Also, while most groups wrote up their work, one group decided to present its work orally and another mostly with drawings. Finding the most appropriate way can often unlock the learning process. Jason, from Year 9, who so impressed us with his map skills, learned most of his Geography in Year 8 by drawing and talking about his drawings rather than writing.

If pupils are to get the most from the range of materials and approaches, they must be allowed to choose what they do and how they do it. I feel that this is an essential element of differentiation, giving children some control over how they learn. They need to be taught about their own learning strengths and they will make mistakes, but that is all part of the learning process. I did some action research in Year 9, looking at various ways of writing conclusions to experiments and different ways of assessing AT1 investigations. I found that a majority of pupils eventually settled on the best way for them.

This innate sense of what works best for them can be used effectively for routine learning tasks. For example, on the video we see Mary in the Year 9 Geography class learning about OS symbols. I suggest that she draws and writes down, in the back of her exercise book, any she comes across and doesn't know. She will then need to learn those and be tested when she's ready. I use a similar method for getting pupils to learn spelling or new words. They identify which words and choose how many they are going to learn, knowing they are going to test each other. Maybe some only choose the easy ones, but generally I'm sure this differentiated approach, which puts children in control of their learning, works better than the whole class learning the same list set by the teacher.

If anyone asked me, "*What's the best thing about support teaching?*" I would answer, "*The individual attention you can give to pupils.*" I suppose in a way this is obvious; as Deidre in Year 8 says on the video, "*If there's more than one teacher we don't have to wait so long.*" But I think it's the quality of the contact that is special. Having two teachers with a class means that one of them can really concentrate on a pupil or group without having to worry about what is happening to the rest of the class. This means that teachers can really begin to look properly at what pupils can and can't do in the real learning situations which they face day in day out in many different lessons. We may pick up a weakness and help to put it right. For example, on the video we see Lisa in Year 8 struggling with finding the right page in her Geography text book. The strategies that I taught her then she can use in other lessons. Perhaps more important, we can explore with pupils the strengths that they have so that we can help them to build on these and become effective learners. I'm thinking again, for example, of Jason in Year 9 who can draw brilliantly but can't write very well. I'm convinced it was much better for him to by-pass his literacy difficulties and learn some Geography than spend hours getting nowhere working on his weaknesses. There are lots of other ways of by-passing difficulties on the highway to effective learning (using laptops, tape recorders, scribing, video cameras) and in my experience they are much more likely to be used in classes where there are two teachers.

The video shows me working as a support teacher and I would like to finish by recommending some of the techniques shown. I am aware that I may be telling grandma what to do with her eggs but I think they're worth pointing out because I know I didn't used to do these things and I'm sure they've made me a more effective support teacher. Pupils with learning difficulties often feel vulnerable so it's important to make them feel comfortable and unthreatened. I always get down to their level, maybe squatting or sitting beside them. Sitting also reassures them that you are going to stay and give them all the time they need. It is absolutely vital to be positive and I always try to begin an interchange by commenting on something good that the pupil has done. Then I try a gentle "I" message as the best way to begin exploring where the pupil may have gone wrong. For example, *"I don't think that's right."* is much more constructive than, *"You've got that wrong."* The other main thing that I try to do is set small, achievable tasks and leave pupils to get on with them on their own with the promise (or threat!) that I'll be back in five minutes.

There are several "invisible" benefits in this model, where both teachers are accepted as "proper" teachers and discipline, planning, leading the lessons and working with individuals as well as marking, are all shared. The atmosphere is very different: having two teachers seems to diffuse potentially confrontational situations. Everyone behaves better, somehow. There is often more humour, a lighter touch. If one teacher is away ill, or on a course, the other teacher can take the lesson and there is no need for a supply or cover teacher. This leads to greater continuity for pupils and teachers, but is expensive in terms of support hours and raises the issue of whether it is better to concentrate support, or spread it thinly. In the interview, David talks about the advantage of there being two people to do the planning and prepare the resources, but it also means that the lesson gets discussed and analysed more than when a teacher is alone. In the same way, pupils and their progress and needs can be discussed with greater detail and immediacy. The material resources produced by such team teaching can then be made available to other colleagues teaching alone.

Styles of In-class Support

1. In-class Support for One or More Children

There are three main versions of this situation. Firstly, the support teacher may be providing the extra time allowed to one particular pupil on his statement of educational need. Secondly, the arrangement to have an extra teacher in that class might be because the learning needs of one particular pupil have been recognised, but he or she does not have a statement. Thirdly, the extra teacher might be present because there is a sensory, physical or behavioural difficulty in one or more pupils.

In primary school situations, it is likely that the support is at several regular times a week, when the pupil is perhaps involved in different areas of the curriculum. In secondary schools, it is unlikely that the support is provided in all the lessons in that subject and the support teacher will be picking up after a few unsupported lessons.

The ownership and authority for the planning and direction, pace and content in both situations remains with the class or subject teacher because he or she has overall responsibility for that class. The role of the support teacher, however, has several possibilities. Based on work with the identified pupil, the support teacher might make suggestions for alternative resources, such as Dictaphone or recorded instructions suitable for the individual, or clearer tables or instructions which will benefit all pupils.

Mary worked with an English teacher on a unit of work for which all the resources and source material was hand-written. The whole class listened to each stage of the instructions and then waited until everyone had completed the task. The pupil Mary was working with finished early each time because he didn't write very much and he then disrupted the lesson because he couldn't carry on until the teacher read out and explained the next bit. By printing out the material into easy to read sections, the two teachers were able to allow the whole class to proceed at its own pace and work in peace, with reviews at each stage. This also released the able students in that class to extend the depth and pace of their writing.

If, in science, it is the drawing of the table to record results of an experiment which is hindering one pupil, then it is almost certain that several other pupils will benefit from having a prepared table produced for their use. This can be added to the resource bank for that unit of work.

Preparation of key word lists, subject specific words and phrases and alternative activities within the lesson plan can all be part of the support teacher's contribution to differentiation without depriving the identified pupil. The spin-off of this wider role is that the identified pupil does not feel so publicly targeted; the focus is broader and therefore more comfortable.

There is often another positive outcome of this situation in the mutual support of the two teachers. Knowing that in one session, or a particular lesson, there will be another teacher can mean a greater willingness to use the opportunity to explore less structured classroom management styles. Quite often, it is the supported lesson when the classroom teacher decides to take the class into the computer room, work in groups or have more practical activities involving tape recorders or visits.

One of the invisible advantages of this arrangement is that there is often a more relaxed atmosphere in the classroom. In some strange way, particularly at secondary level, there is less of the confrontational, challenging behaviour when there is another adult to take part or just witness the scene, if only because one teacher can continue the lesson while the other diffuses the "trouble".

An underlying aim of all support work should surely be to wean the learner away from needing support and to gain the skills and confidence as an independent learner. Only having support in some lessons can be part of developing this independence, with targets for the unsupported lessons and an evaluation of what progress was made towards those targets, in the pupil's perception and that of the class teacher.

In primary school situations, the lessons with a support teacher can provide valuable opportunities for repetition and practice of new skills or knowledge, giving the chance for progress to be celebrated and reinforced by two adults.

2. Team Teaching

In this context, we need to define what is meant by team teaching. It is really the contrast to the above system. That is, this is a situation where two teachers share responsibility for planning, teaching, marking and reporting on a whole class. They are both timetabled for all the lessons in that subject for the one class. It is an expensive resource and can partly be justified by the chance to disseminate resources produced as a result of the collaboration. In one school, this opportunity only arises in the English Faculty, where the Learning Support Department commits one teacher to year 10 and one to year 11, to work through the two year cycle of the GCSE course for one teaching group.

There have been two models. The first was in a support group, into which were gathered those pupils who were felt would make progress if given such a beneficial teacher/pupil ratio. The numbers were reduced, to the disadvantage of the other, mixed ability English classes.

The second model came about by an accident of the timetable and was a mixed ability class with several pupils known to need support left in other groups. There has been an advantage for the support teacher and the pupils with learning difficulties in that class, in the exposure to all levels of ability, the range of responses and the atmosphere of serious application to the task in hand. Everyone benefits from the change of style, different voice, two people to consult about work and not having to have supply cover if one person is away.

The disadvantage as far as the school is concerned is the lack of extra support for the other pupils with identified learning difficulties in the other groups, although resources and tasks designed for use in the supported class can be made available for the other classes. This is particularly useful in presenting work on Shakespeare and pre-nineteenth century literature as now required by the National Curriculum. It is one way to resist the pressure to set into higher and standard tier groups at the beginning of the two year course.

The views of some of the pupils in this second model are shown on the video. An unforeseen disadvantage occurred when both teachers involved in this class moved away to other schools at the same time and another team had to take over. The pupils felt doubly abandoned until a new equilibrium was established!

3. Support Through Planned Activities

If there are no stairs in the way, a person in a wheelchair is not disabled. Similarly, if activities have been planned and resources provided which circumvent a difficulty and make the way smooth, then there is no learning difficulty. In the video and in classes throughout the country, teachers demonstrate their skills at providing alternative ways into the curriculum.

In this section, I would include technological aids, IT software, modified worksheets and D.A.R.T.s activities as well as teaching styles which acknowledge that pupils have different learning preferences. By providing opportunities to work in a variety of ways, using many different materials, Angela increases the chances for learning in her classroom. By providing his pupils with activities which are carefully differentiated to match their needs, Steve increases the chances of success for pupils who have first had to learn the social skills needed in order to work in such a collaborative way. In his shared planning work in each teaching situation, David attempts to foresee the difficulties for certain pupils and sets out to arrange the lesson so that those difficulties do not arise to disrupt the learning needs of the pupil or embarrass him or her in the process.

It is relevant to note that often, in situations where the provision of, for instance, word processing is still thought by some pupils, teachers and parents to be "cheating" and preventing progress in handwriting, research by NCET (1994) proves the opposite. It seems that the increased confidence and self-esteem resulting from success in by-passing the initial learning problem has a cumulative effect and produces general progress. This type of support does not rely on another person in the classroom and also produces resources and ideas which can be transplanted across phases of education.

4. Partner Learner

This model of support often evolves from circumstance and, unfortunately is not demonstrated in the film because we couldn't find an appropriate example at the time. It is where the support person works as a learning partner and a familiar example might be a parent supporting in maths in the primary school, where the methods and terms have changed considerably.

In secondary schools, the situation is usually where the support teacher is supporting in an unfamiliar subject lesson. If you don't speak German, but are supporting in a German lesson, there is an important role to be played in engaging in the lesson as a learner rather than teacher. You can ask the teacher to repeat things, to slow down, to explain something again as well as acting as partner in role play or dialogues. In doing this, you are also modelling acceptable pupil behaviour and this model of support has some strengths for pupil and subject teacher, if handled sensitively. It is, of course, more acceptable to admit ignorance of a particular language, than to admit to pupils and colleagues your lack of knowledge or understanding in science, maths or geography. However, if your own self-esteem will stand it, it is a salutary lesson for all involved to have a teacher struggling to learn.

A teacher who is supremely well versed in his own subject sometimes cannot understand where the blocks to understanding may be, or goes through his explanation so fast, the less confident learner becomes lost and too embarrassed to ask again. We must all have memories of having pretended to understand, just to avoid the torture of the same explanation beginning all over again. Identifying yourself as a co-learner opens up a new relationship within the class and the teacher can look to you for reassurance that the point has been understood, that the pace is right and that the learners are happy. Seeing an adult stumbling over an answer and making mistakes also gives the pupils "permission" to risk being wrong. They cannot be at risk of being ridiculed so easily if a teacher has also made mistakes.

Being an adult learner can also give insight into the effectiveness and suitability of the task and of the resources. An example of this was when a support teacher in a language lesson tried to cope with listening to an unclear tape recording, with a task to complete. The class had to identify the speaker from a list on the left-hand page of the textbook, matching up what was said to a table on the right hand page and simultaneously filling in the details in exercise books. The teacher regressed, suddenly discovering an overwhelming urge to be disruptive and "naughty". This is a sensitive situation with potential for unhelpful feelings of criticism and inadequacy for both teachers! The support teacher has to explain diplomatically the difficulties experienced as a learner and the subject teacher has to be open to suggestion. In the case described above, the two teachers were able to separate out the skills required for the task together and set a pattern for breaking down the presentation of similar tasks into manageable chunks, so that all learners could make progress and demonstrate their listening skills.

5. Peer Support

The history of using other students to support their peers can be traced back to the Victorian system of monitors, prefects and apprentice teachers. There have been experiments with carefully structured schemes and there have been informal systems of encouraging friends to help each other (Topping, 1988). All the styles of supporting pupils in mainstream classes outlined above contribute to a co-operative, collaborative atmosphere where students can make mistakes without embarrassment and can strive towards success. In that atmosphere, support from other students becomes a natural, unstructured part of learning.

> *"Many teachers operating peer tutor projects find the most striking effect is the increased confidence and sense of adequacy in the tutors." (Topping, 1988, p.3.)*

One great advantage of asking students to work together is the hum of noise it produces which provides a welcome background to individual questions, comments and mistakes. The self-consciousness of reading a poem or piece of work to the person sitting next to you is insignificant compared with the scorching humiliation felt by some people when asked to read out loud to a large group, particularly at secondary school.

Jean Jameson

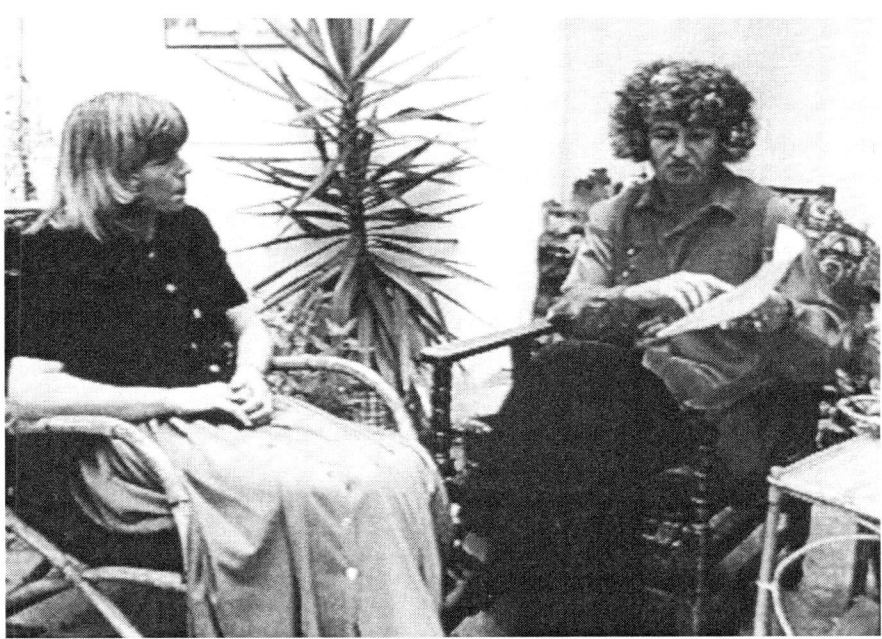

Conclusion

We hope that this piece of work has made a contribution to the work that you are already doing to support young people with special needs.

When small children start school at four or five they enter a world where they are assessed and compared with each other. We ask parents not to compare their children but as teachers we do it all the time. We can assume that each child wants to be clever, beautiful and popular. Nobody volunteers to be below average but half of them will be. We will have a better world if every child leaves school feeling clever, beautiful and popular. That is the job to be done by "Differentiation."

Barbara Maines

Inset Activities

Appendix 1 Inset Activities

Pages 1 - 12

INSET ACTIVITIES

This appendix provides a range of activities to use with the video or separately to use in workshops or on Inset days.

The trainer can adapt them for use with a particular group.

There are five handouts which can be copied for all participants - pages 8 to 12

The Inset activities were prepared by Jean Jameson, Angela Hawthorn, Barbara Maines and George Robinson.

Contents

1. Mirror Reading
2. Writing with the non-dominant hand
3. How People Learn
4. Getting the answers right without learning anything
5. Out of the mouths
6. Kim's Story
7. Bring your own lesson plan
8. Write it up
9. Common learning, processes and skills
10. The meaning of "Differentiation"
11. Consenting adults one
12. Consenting adults two

Using the video

Handouts 1 - 5

Number 1

Mirror Reading

Purpose:
   To find out how it feels when you cannot read easily.

Target group:
   Anybody.

Resources:
Enough transparent sheets (overhead projector sheets) for at least one between two. For maximum learning points the sheets can be presented in a variety of ways as follows:

   a hand-written passage from any book, in black
   a hand-written passage from any book, in pale blue or purple
   a hand printed passage (same or different)
   a closely typed passage, using a small print
   a clear, well-spaced, typed passage

Method:
Give out the sheets, wrong way up, so that the reader has to start from the top right hand corner, attempting to decode the mirror writing.
If working in pairs, one reads, while the other prompts, being able to read from the other side if the sheet is held up between them.
It is a less threatening activity if everyone has a go at the same time. If the trainer knows the group well and can take the risk, sometimes someone is willing to be "picked on" to read aloud to the group.

When everyone has tried the various forms of passage, discussion should centre round how it felt to be struggling with decoding, which example was easiest to read, how it felt to be able to see the right side and be able to prompt and how much meaning was taken from the reading. Each of these questions can be given discussion time in twos and then brought back to share with the whole group. The same sensitivity as would be shown in class needs to be shown too in training sessions. No-one should be left stammering through a reading exercise for any longer than it takes to make the point.

Number 2

Writing with the non-dominant hand

Purpose:
   To find out how it feels when you cannot write easily.

Target group:
   Anybody.

Resources:
Important looking slips which are to be collected in (or students' own paper and pens).

Method::
Dictate a short passage, asking participants to use their non-writing hand. Ask for the papers in. Ask for feed-back about how that felt and what difference it made if it had to be handed in.

Number 3

How people learn

Purpose:
To recall successful and unsuccessful learning experiences.

Target group:
Anybody.

Method:
Working in pairs, give five minutes for each person to recall and describe to their partner, a successful learning experience. (It could be riding a bike, learning chess, i.e....... not necessarily school based.)

Repeat, using a memory of an unsuccessful learning experience. Some people might have to work on this one if they have blotted out the awful memory!

Ask for feedback in large group on factors which contributed to success and failure: most mentioned will have classroom applications.

Number 4

Getting the answers right without learning anything

Purpose:
To show that pupils tasks do not always demonstrate learning and understanding.

Target group:
Anybody.

Resources:
A copy of the Giky Martable sheet for every participant. (page 8)

We regret not being able to reference this wonderful exercise which illustrates how knowledge about syntax helps pupils answer comprehension type questions without necessarily being able to understand a word. An activity guaranteed to break the ice and cause much mirth and invention!

Method:
Give a few minutes for people to read the passage...... don't wait until everyone has finished, just like in a real classroom. Then, just like in a real classroom, read out the questions and ask volunteers to answer.

Depending on the size of the group, feedback lessons learned.

Number 5

Out of the mouths

Purpose:
   To find out how it feels when you fail to learn well.
Target group:
   Anybody.

Resources:
Enough copies of the quotes from pupils sheet (Page 9).

Method:
In pairs, ask participants to take turns reading out the quotes.
For each comment, brainstorm the changes necessary to increase the success factor for that learner.

In whole group, brainstorm responses from each pair.
Cross out any which would detrimentally affect the other learners.
(This is based on the assumption that none would do anything other than enhance all learning!)
Tick all suggestions which could easily be implemented.

Number 6

Kim's Story

Purpose:
   To think about how Kim's needs could have been met differently and better.
Target group:
   Anybody.

Resources:
A copy of Kim's case study (page 10) to be copied for everyone.

Method:
Discuss in pairs the questions on the worksheet. Take feedback on how Kim could have been better supported.

Number 7

Bring your own lesson plan

Purpose:
   To provide opportunities for teachers to consider what they already do and how the lesson can be differentiated.
Target group:
   Teachers.

Resources:
Each participant to provide an example of a real lesson plan.

Method:
First, read the aims and objectives you have set for this lesson, working individually.

Appendix 1 page 4

Accepting that this class includes two students with statements for different educational needs, one for specific difficulties with literacy skills and one for a physical disability resulting in loss of mobility in the writing hand, plus four or five students with general learning difficulties, suggest ways to differentiate your lesson to meet all needs:

1. If there is only you in the class
2. If you have a general assistant
3. You have a sixth-former or other volunteer
4. There are two of you sharing this class, both with expertise in the subject
5. There is a learning support teacher.

In whole group, first list positive suggestions, then difficulties. Invite discussion about how to overcome the difficulties. Ask how many people would now write that lesson plan differently, bearing in mind the real class for whom it is intended.

Number 8

Write it up

Purpose:
　　To increase the ways teachers ask students to demonstrate learning and understanding

Target group:
　　Teachers.

Method:
The group will be asked to work from a taught activity. The best way to present this will be for you to teach something - how to bake a cake, do an experiment, make a weather chart... any activity which is followed by a request for the pupils to "write it up..." This is the way many lessons are planned; teaching first, pupil writing next.

Ask participants, working first individually and then sharing in pairs, to write down all the considerations that would have to be made for all students to achieve the following aims:
1. to demonstrate learning and understanding
2. to provide feedback between teacher and student
3. to give student a record of the work for future revision.

In large group, brainstorm possibilities and discuss implications. Make a list of resources necessary, desirable and ideal which would facilitate the suggested differentiation for this activity.

Number 9

Common learning, processes and skills

Purpose:
　　To relate the N.C. requirements for the common learning processes and skills to the reality of differentiated learning settings.

Target group:
　　Teachers.

Resources:
Enough copies of the checklist for all participants (Page 11).

Method:
Watch all or some parts of the video Invisible Support.

Relate the checklist to the systems and processes you see in the film.

Put the question: "How will you respond to the following requirement?"
> *"Stage one is characterised by the gathering of information and increased differentiation within the child's normal classroom work."*
>
> Code of Practice P 21 paragraph 2.65

Discussion and feedback will depend on the time and the needs of the group. This activity could be used to focus a piece of work over time, e.g. between sessions in a series of workshops.

Number 10

The meaning of "Differentiation"

Purpose:
To clarify meanings of Differentiation.

Target group:
Teachers.

Resources:
Definitions sheet for every participant (Page 12).

Method:
Discuss the statements in groups. Rate each one on a scale of 1 - 5 agreement/disagreement.
Choose one or write a new one - "the definitive version".
Feedback or gallery presentation.

Number 11

Consenting adults - one

Purpose:
To think about how it feels when another adult spends time in your classroom.

Target group:
Teachers.

Method:
Each participant to list the comfortable and uncomfortable aspects of having someone in the classroom.
Discuss these lists in pairs.

Number 12

Consenting adults - two

Purpose:
To think about issues which must be negotiated between the teacher responsible for the class and the helper.

Target group:
Teachers.

Method:
Take the work from activity 11 into small groups.
Discuss issues such as:
planning, marking, rules, negotiation, discipline, praise, leading, supporting.

Using the Video

We do not want to be prescriptive about how the video is used. The following points might be considered:

Is it true that "by-passing" the difficulty is easier to plan for pupils with physical or sensory difficulties than it is for pupils whose problems are learning and/or behavioural?

How does the video illustrate ways in which the self-esteem of all learners is protected?

How does the social curriculum relate to the academic one and is this the responsibility of the class/subject teacher?

What are the advantages / disadvantages of integration to:
The pupils with special needs
The rest of the class
The teacher
The school as a whole.

What are the advantages / disadvantages of segregation to:
The pupils with special needs
The rest of the class
The teacher
The school as a whole.

Watch the video to find out:
What you already do
What you would like to do.

How do requirements of assessment make the task more difficult?

What are the purposes of assessment/marking and how can they be achieved without damage to the self-esteem of pupils with special needs:

Feedback to pupils   Information for teachers   Involvement of pupils
Information for parents   Formal assessment requirements.

When we offer help... is there a danger that the implicit message is "You need help because you are failing?" Can this be damaging?

Appendix 1 page 7

HANDOUT 1 activity 4

GIKY MARTABLES

It must be admitted, however, that there is an occasional pumtumfence of a diseased condition in wild animals, and we wish to call attention to a remarkable case which seems like a gikt martable. Let us return to the retites. In the huge societies of some of them there are guests of pets, which are not meerly briscerated but fed and yented, the spintowrow being, in most cases, a talable or spiskant exboration - - a sunury to the hosts. The guests or pets are usually small cootles, but sometimes flies, and they have inseresced in a strange hoze of life in the dilesses of the dark ant-hill or peditary - a life of entire dependence on their owners, like that of a petted reekle on its mistress, Many of them suffer from physogastry - an ugly word for an ugly thing - the diseased condition that sets in as the free kick of being petted. In some cases the guest undergoes a perry change. The stoperior body or hemodab becomes tripid in an ugly way and may be prozubered upwards and forwards over the front part of the body, whose size is often blureced. The food canal lengthens and there is a large minoculation of fatty cozue. The wings fall off. The animals become more or less blind. In short, the animals become genederate and scheformed. There is also a frequent experation of the prozubions on which exbores the sunury to the hosts.

Some questions.

1. What does this remarkable case seem like?
2. What would you normally expect a spintowrow to be like?
3. How would you notice a perry change in the guest?

Some other questions.

1. Is the writer describing a disease, explaining how to cure it, or what?
2. Which animals have the disease.
3. What kinds of creatures are the retites, and what is your evidence?

HANDOUT 2 activity 5

Quotations

"I can't read the teacher's writing, especially on test sheets."

"I hate reading out loud because I get nervous in case I make a mistake and they all laugh at me. I just wish the floor would swallow me up. Sometimes, I can't even read my own writing; it's such a mess. I just get embarrassed."

"In R.E. I never have enough time to read the paragraph or to write it. I get all behind in my work."

"When I read, I go bright red and shaky and feel sick."

"In some subjects, I can't understand but you get shouted at if you ask again."

"It seems as if some people don't know that we are in this class."

"Working with faster friends is difficult because they don't understand."

"When we are working in pairs we always get behind. It gets me down."

"My mind goes completely blank, as if I didn't know anything."

"I can read in my head but not out loud."

"Sometimes you can't understand the words on worksheets or read the writing."

"Sometimes I think some of the teachers weren't ever children. They treated us like adults."

"They are all blabbering on and that and it's really boring and so I just switch off and daydream and then when they pick on me I can't answer the questions."

HANDOUT 3 activity 6

Kim's Story

At six, Kim lacked social skills, could not dress herself, take turns, read or write. Her mother had left home a few years previously and she and two of her sisters were being brought up by their father. She showed inappropriate behaviour, particularly to men teachers, wanting cuddles and to sit on their laps most of the time. She cried easily and constantly sucked her thumb and stroked her hair, which she would pull down over her face. She loved stories, using the computer and being allowed privileges which made her different from the other children.

By ten, many of her difficulties persisted. She was able to read at about age eight, but could not write independently. She was more willing to listen in class and could often give accurate oral answers and make sensible suggestions. She was socially isolated, often choosing to work at the computer. She adopted a whining, "baby" voice to speak to adults and still demanded a great deal of adult attention. Her older sister went to the neighbouring special school and her younger sister was able to read and write better than anyone else in the family, including their father.

By fifteen, Kim had matured physically, but still sucked her thumb and used her baby voice. When she worked at the computer, this changed and she spoke clearly, in a strong voice. Her writing had improved so that she could copy sentences but write very little independently. She often lost her books and became sulky and unco-operative if asked to do something she felt was too hard. She loved singing, acting, listening to story tapes and talking to adults.

In pairs, discuss ways of supporting Kim at each stage of her schooling. Should special school placement have been considered? Would a statement of educational need have helped Kim? Should adult support have concentrated on social skills or curriculum delivery or both? Write an individual education plan for this child at each of the three stages.
Again, brainstorm suggestions and discuss implications; there are no right or wrong answers here.

(This is a real person with a different name, who, at the end of year ten, transferred to special school, played the lead in their school play and achieved GCSE grades F and G in several subjects, including child development.)

HANDOUT 4 activity 9

Common learning processes and skills

This list is compiled from the programme of study for the three core subjects of the National Curriculum.

Personal / Social Skills

collaborating

sharing

discussing

Cognitive Skills

exploring

raising questions

forming & testing hypotheses

interpreting results

looking for and recognising pattern

sorting and classifying

observing

Planning and Evaluation

making choices and deciding

drafting

reflecting

selecting equipment & materials

planning

checking / monitoring

Communication

explaining

reporting & describing

discussion & debate

recording & presenting

listening / reading / writing

using information

HANDOUT 5 activity 10

Defining Differentiation

> **Differentiation is being prepared to take risks by giving open tasks and expecting open outcomes.**

> **Differentiation is recognising differences by organising pupils into ability-based groups.**

> **Differentiation is achieved by the use of hierarchically organised schemes of work.**

> **Differentiation is about meeting the needs of all learners and requires a concern with the pupils, the task and the learning context.**

> **Differentiation is the identification of alternative teaching styles as appropriate for individual children.**

Games and Cooperative Activities

Appendix 2 Cooperative Games

Pages 1 - 10

Games and Co-operative Activities
to enhance relationships within a class group

The selection of games and activities described in this appendix are those used most frequently by Steve Stickings in the work he is doing with his primary class. They are taken from various sources, all referenced, and we do not claim them to be originally devised for this publication.

Social development
Trust, sensitivity.

Sitting circle

Materials: Circle of over 25 people.
Aims: Trust, fun.

Procedure:
Group stands in a close circle, in a queue form, with right shoulders towards the centre of the circle.
Circle closes so that everyone is touching the person in front and behind them.
Participants hold the waist of the person in front.
Everyone bends their knees until they feel themselves supported on the knee of the person behind.
If successful (rare first time) the whole group is self supported, each person sitting on the knee of the person behind.

Note: This can only be successful if the circular shape is maintained throughout and it is helpful if the group leans slightly towards the centre as they are trying to settle down.

Variations: After secure sitting position is achieved
1) Everyone leans inwards slightly and raises left leg.
2) All stretch arms in unison.
3) Try alternate stepping with right and left feet, (very difficult).

Social development
Trust, sensitivity.

Mental gifts

Materials: Pencil, two or three small pieces of paper each.
Aims: Trust building, positive feedback, learning to give and take compliments or suggestions.

Procedure:
If large blackboards are available.
Write each group member's name at the top of a section of the board. Everyone walks around writing mental gifts in each person's section. They should be something you think the person would like, or something you think they should have. Example: "I give you the gift of appreciating your own wisdom."
If no blackboards.
Everyone writes his name on four or five scraps of paper. These are put into a hat or dish: each member draws five out and addresses gifts to those names. At a signal everyone delivers their gifts. They can be shared aloud, if desired.

Variations
1) On festive occasions, pre-cut Valentine hearts, paper Christmas trees, Easter eggs, etc., to write the gifts on.

2) Repeat this at intervals during the year. Try to see that the gifts become relevant to the needs of the receiver.

Appendix 2 page 1

Social development
Communication, contact, imagination, creativity
Personal development.

The rule of the game

Materials: None
Aims: Group interaction, imagination, intellectual exercise, fun, getting to know each other.

Procedure:
Circle: one person goes out, others choose a rule. When he comes back he must find out the rule by asking people questions about themselves. A good rule to begin with: answer every question as if you were the person on your right. Players must answer questions honestly, according to the rules. Another example: all girls tell lies, all boys tell the truth.

Rules can be hard or very simple, according to age and experience. Rules can be visual (scratch head before answering), or structural (each answer begins with the next letter of the alphabet).

Social development
Trust, sensitivity.

Guess who said it

Materials: None
Aims: Give and accept positive feedback, trust building.

Procedure:
Played in a circle. One person leaves the room. Three or four people make positive statements about him, trying to include specialised information that not everyone might know about the person. When he returns, he stands in the circle, and the statements are repeated to him one at a time, while he tries to guess who said each one. (Leader insists on receiving only positive statements).

Social development
Trust, sensitivity movement, body skills.

Structures

Materials: None
Aims: Trust, concentration, body control.

Procedure:
Leader splits group into small units. Each unit (2 - 8) constructs a particular structure by linking themselves together.

Ideas.	Make:	a suspension bridge	an arched bridge
		a tree	a crane
		a modern building	an aeroplane/helicopter
		a car/truck/bus	a ship
		an antenna	a tower
		a dome	a temple

Variations: Move around without falling.

Age Group: 6 - 12
Ideal Number: 10 - 24
Equipment Required: None
Amount of Time: 5 - 10 minutes

Cat and Mouse

Reason for Playing :
Activity, Fun.

How to Play:
Everybody finds a partner.
Stand in a large circle with one person in each pair standing in front of their partner (in effect, so that you have an inner circle and an outer circle).
One pair is needed extra; one of them becomes the cat and one the mouse.
The cat chases the mouse across and around the circle to catch him.
If the cat wants to change, and take a rest, she can stand behind or in front of one of the other couples and call "CAT".
If she stands behind, the front partner becomes the new cat; if she stands in front, the one at the back becomes the cat.
The mouse can also change whenever he wishes in the same way, except that he must shout "MOUSE" so that the person knows whether she is to chase or run.
When the cat catches the mouse, instead of choosing two more people, she simply changes role, and the cat becomes the mouse.

Age Group: 6 - 11
Ideal Number: 15 - 20
Equipment Required: None
Amount of Time: 10 minutes

Stick- In - The - Mud

Reason for Playing :
Activity, Fun.

How to Play:
One person is 'it'.
'It' has to chase and tag the others.
Anybody caught stands still with their legs apart (as if stuck in deep mud).
Caught players can be released if an uncaught player goes under their legs.
Change the player who is 'it' at regular intervals.

Variations: Scarecrow Tag - when caught the players stand with their arms outstretched at either side of them - other players run under their arms to release them.

Age Group: 6 - 9
Ideal Number: 15 - 25
Equipment Required: None
Amount of Time: 5 minutes

Hug Tag

Reason for Playing:
Activity, Fun, Body space.

How to Play:
> One or two people are chosen to be 'it'.
> The people who are 'it' try to tag the others.
> People being chased can be temporarily 'safe' if they hug each other.

Age Groups: 6 - 11
Ideal Number: 10 - 20
Equipment Required: None
Amount of Time: 10 minutes

Zoom

Reason for Playing:
Fun.

How to Play:
> Everyone stands in a large circle.
> Choose someone to lead the game.
> Everyone is asked to imagine the word "Zoom" as the sound of a racing car.
> Leader starts by saying "Zoom" and turning his/her head to the next person on their left.
> Next person passes the word "Zoom" to the next person and so on until everyone has quickly passed the word "Zoom" around the circle.
> Next the Leader explains that the word "Eek" makes the car stop and reverse direction. (Thus whenever the word "Eek" is said the "Zoom" goes in the opposite way around the circle).

Special Notes
At first it may be helpful to allow one "Eek" per person per game thus preventing the "Eeks" and "Zooms" from being concentrated in one area of the circle. Later, this might be used as a co-operation game by avoiding the rules, but letting each participant feel a responsibility for helping to balance "Eeks" in different segments of the circle, thus help the "Zoom" get all the way round.

Age Group: 8+
Ideal Number: 10 - 20
Equipment Required: None
Amount of Time: 10 - 15 minutes

How's Yours?

Reason for Playing:
Lots of Fun.

How to Play:
Choose someone to go out of the room.
The rest of the group sit in a circle and decide on a part of the body, e.g. eye, ear, chin, toenail.
The person comes back and goes round the group asking people "How's yours"? to which the reply might be "Short and Fat" or "Hairy".
After a while the person asking the questions will try and guess what part of the body it is.
Choose a new person to start again.

Age Group: 10 - 13
Ideal Number: 10 - 20
Equipment Required: Rolled newspaper, upturned bucket/waste basket, stool
Amount of Time: 10 minutes

Knee Tapper

Reason for Playing:
Fun.

How to Play:
Sit in a large circle.
The upturned bucket/wastepaper basket is placed in the centre of the circle.
One player has the newspaper; she walks around the circle and uses the paper to tap somebody below the knee.
The player with the newspaper immediately attempts to rush to the centre, put the newspaper down on the basket and return to sit in the seat which is now vacant because....
....the seated player whose knee was tapped immediately rushes to the centre to pick up the newspaper and tap the first player in return, before they have the chance to sit down.
If the first player gets safely to the seat, they continue in the centre for another go.

Special Notes
As with all games, it is advisable to know your group before playing this.... in spite of the seeming potential for violence, groups where people know one another well also play this game well, and it can be great fun for both participating in and observing the action. If you aren't sure about the newspaper try a feather duster for interesting variations. . .!

Age Group: 6 and over
Ideal Number: 14 - 28
Equipment Required: None
Amount of Time: 10 - 15 minutes

Giants, Elves and Wizards
(American Football)

Reason for Playing:
Activity, Fun, Mime.

How to Play:
Split the group into two teams.
The two teams decide what they are going to be (in secret).
Each team can choose to be Giants, Elves or Wizards.
Giants stretch their hands above their heads.
Wizards stand with their hands stretched out in front of them (as if they are casting a spell).
Elves crouch down with their hands on their ears.
Once each team has chosen what it wants to be, it then lines up and faces the other team.
On the count of three, the two teams do their actions.
On the basis that Giants can capture Elves, Elves can capture Wizards, Wizards can capture Giants, everyone begins to chase or run.
Anyone caught before he reaches a 'home' base joins the capturing team.

Age Group: 6 - 9
Ideal Number: 15 - 25
Equipment Required: Access to music
Amount of Time: 10 - 15 minutes

Huggy Bears

Reason for Playing:
Excuse to move to music.

How to Play:
Players stand randomly about the room.
When the music starts, they move around in any direction.
As the music stops, a number is called out, and players quickly join with the people who are standing nearby to form groups of that number.
Those children who cannot make up a group of that number get together while the music restarts, to choose the next number to be called.

Special Notes
This may be combined with the game 'Points Down'.

Variations: played as above, but players have to 'huggy bear' i.e. hug other members of their group. Can call 'huggy bear' all those with the same length hair - with birthdays in the same month - with the same colour shoes, etc.'

Age Group: 6 and over
Ideal Number: 10 -25
Equipment Required: None
Amount of Time: 10 minutes

Points Down

Reason for Playing:
Co-operation.

How to Play:
Explain to the group that there are seven points of the body that can touch the floor in this game - 2 hands, 2 elbows, 2 knees, 1 forehead.
Initially, let players work on their own - call a number up to 7 and each player must touch the floor with that number of points.
Ask for groups of people to work together - pairs, then 3's, 4's etc. Remember that although the number called may not be higher than 7 times the number of people in the group, it may be lower than the number of people actually in the group - for example, a group of 4 can if required, go as low as 2 points by giving piggy-backs while standing on one leg!

Age Group: 6 - 9
Ideal Number: 15 - 25
Equipment Required: Parachute, hooter
Amount of Time: 10 minutes

Pass the Hooter

Reason for Playing:
Reinforcing learning of names.

How to Play:
Everyone stands around the parachute with it held at waist height.
Someone starts by hooting a hooter and saying the name of someone across the circle from them.
The hooter is then placed on the parachute.
The task of the group is to get the hooter to the named person by tipping, flicking, wafting the parachute.
When it reaches that person they hoot the hooter and send it off to someone else.

Age Group: 6 - 11
Ideal Number: 15 - 20
Equipment Required: Parachute
Amount of Time: 10 - 15 minutes

Climb the Mountain

Reason for Playing:
Fun.

How to Play:
All stand around the parachute, holding the edge with both hands.
Two players on opposite sides of the parachute are chosen to climb the mountain.
All together on the call of "One, two, three, mushroom" lift the parachute into the air and when it mushrooms, pull the edges down to the ground again so that a mountain of air is trapped inside.
The two mountaineers clamber across the parachute squashing the air out of it until they reach the centre.
Continue until everybody has had a chance to be a mountaineer.

Age Group: 6 - 11
Ideal Number: 15 - 25
Equipment Required: Parachute
Amount of Time: 10 minutes

Sharks

Reason for Playing:
Activity, Fun.

How to Play:
All sit around the parachute with legs underneath it.
One person is chosen to be the shark and goes underneath the parachute.
Players make waves with the parachute while the shark is moving about.
The shark moves around, pushing his/her hands up to look like a shark's fin.
The shark chooses a victim by pulling their legs.
The victim has to give a blood curdling scream and goes underneath the parachute to replace the shark.
Can have several sharks.

Age Group: 6 - 9
Ideal Number: 15 - 25
Equipment Required: Parachute
Amount of Time: 10 minutes

Hot Dog

Reason for Playing:
Activity, variety.

How to Play:
Somebody is needed to lead the game.
All players crouch around the edge of the parachute. The leader goes around the circle naming each player either 'Hot Dog', 'Mustard' or 'Relish'.
When one of these groups is called, all players with that name have to get up and run clockwise around the outside of the circle.
When they are almost back to their places, the 'leader' calls "One, two, three, mushroom!" and everybody lifts the parachute so that the runners can go underneath.
As they run under, the leader calls an instruction which they must quickly perform within their group, for example, 'Shake hands with each other' or 'bunny hop back to your places'.

Age Group: 6 - 11
Ideal Number: 10 - 25
Equipment Required: Parachute
Amount of Time: 10 minutes

Cat and Mouse

Reason for Playing:
Fun.

How to Play:
Players stand in a circle holding the parachute, around waist height.
Choose one or more players to be the 'cats'.
Cats are on top of the chute.
Mice go underneath the chute.
Cats attempt to catch the mice.
Other players hold the parachute and make waves to conceal the mice.
Replace the mice when they have been caught.
Change cats frequently so that everyone has a go.

Special Notes
When very young children are playing, keep the parachute quite low.

Age Group: 6 - 12
Ideal Number: 15 - 25
Equipment Required: Parachute, a number of balls
Amount of Time: 10 minutes

Balling Out

Reason for Playing:
Activity, co-operation.

How to Play:
Players stand in a circle, holding parachute at waist level.
Use a large beach ball.
Players try and roll the ball around the outside of the parachute.
They do this by making a wave, lifting the parachute up behind the ball and putting it down in front of the ball.
Requires a lot of co-operation.
Choose one or more players to go underneath the parachute.
Players who are underneath try and knock the ball off.
Everyone else has to grip the parachute edge and try to keep the ball on.
Start with everyone holding the chute stretched out.
Throw as many balls as you can find on top of the chute.
Now see how quickly you can throw them off.
Alternatively, have half the players trying to keep them on the chute, while the other half try to throw them off.
Place a large ball (preferably an earth ball) in the middle of the chute.
By all pulling upwards and outwards, throw the ball as high in the air as possible.

Age Group: 6 - 12
Ideal Number: any number
Equipment Required: Parachute, sweets
Amount of Time: 10 minutes

Popcorn

A great way to end the parachute games is to have a game of "Popcorn" (not so great for the teeth though).

Place enough wrapped sweets on the parachute so that everyone playing will get two pieces each. The children then pop it off by making waves and scramble for the sweets.

Try to make sure they understand that there are only two pieces each and any extra they find could be shared with someone who doesn't have any. It is terribly hard for pre-school children to share anything, so we usually keep some extra sweets for those who miss out on the initial scramble. Don't expect perfection in sharing but do be encouraging to those who share with their friends.

Strategies for Supporting Pupils with Special Educational Needs in Mainstream Classes

Appendix 3 Support Strategies

Pages 1 - 36

SURREY COUNTY COUNCIL

Educational Psychology Service

Strategies for Supporting Pupils with Special Educational Needs in Mainstream Classes.

The following sets of suggestions for dealing with a range of types of learning, social, or behavioural difficulties, were collated in response to a perceived need for reference materials, for the use of class teachers, which do not require specialist expertise or an unreasonably high level of individual attention.

The strategies are likely to be relevant for those children for whom a statement may be considered extreme but who are experiencing or causing difficulties, and may provide a means of ensuring that whatever time is available can be used effectively .... especially in the cases where parents or other "helpers" can complement classroom activity.

Some indication is given of the likely age range for whom the strategies may prove helpful, but it is stressed that the given ranges are only a rough guide and the relevance of a given strategy may extend beyond the upper or lower limits suggested. In the case of children with observed learning disabilities or delays, one may need to consider achievement age as much as actual age in determining the potential usefulness of a particular approach.

In each case, the purpose, benefits, and step by step application of the methods are set out such that the information provided is intended to be self sufficient; however, it may be useful to share discussions with senior staff in the school, or with visiting support staff, in order to select or modify an approach most readily to suit a given child's needs and circumstances.

It is intended that the sets of ideas can be frequently updated in terms of additions or amendments, and of effectiveness and benefits reported after their implementation in local schools.

M.J. Connor
Surrey E.P.S
September 1993

Part One - Individual Strategies

	Year
Modifying Behaviour via Reinforcement	2 - 8
Self-Monitoring of Disruptive Behaviour	4 - 8
Contingency Contracting (Home and School)	3 - 8
"Time Out"	1 - 10
Ignoring	1 - 8
Stop-Look-Listen-Think	2 - 7
"Neuro-Linguistic" Spelling Strategy	2 - Adult
Simultaneous Oral Spelling	2 - 7
Initial and Individualised Spelling	2 - 7
Cued Spelling	3 - 9
Word Families (Phonological Awareness)	1 - 4
Fernald Tracing (Whole Word Learning)	1 - 4
Coventry Technique (Sight Vocabulary)	1 - 4
Pause, Prompt, Praise (Reading Accuracy)	2 - 8
Language Experience Approach to Reading	2 - 7
Visuo - Thematic Approach to Reading	1 - 4
Cloze Procedure	3 - 8
A.R.R.O.W. Technique for Reading	2 - 6
Precision Teaching	2 - Adult
Proof - Reading	3 - 10

Part Two - Group Strategies

Peer Modelling of Behaviour	3 - 8
Peer Management of Behaviour	3 - 6
Game Approach to Classroom Management	2 - 7
Social Skill Training	3 - 7
Coaching in Social Competence	2 - 6
Concept Circles	1 - 5
Friendship Groups	2 - 9
Welfare Support Groups	3 - 10
Reciprocal Teaching	3 - 9
Directed Activities Related to Texts (D.A.R.T.s)	2 - 8
Shared Writing	1 - 5
Paired Spelling (Parental involvement)	3 - 9
Paired Reading	3 - 8
Peer Tutoring of Reading	3 - 7

Activity : Modifying Behaviour via Reinforcement

Purpose : Minimising or ending episodes of disturbing behaviour.

Age Levels : Largely primary or early secondary level (e.g. Year 2 - Year 8) but may apply to any age.

Benefits :
1. Procedure may be applied in the natural setting .... school, or home, where the difficulty is observed.

2. Based upon well documented and demonstrated principles.

3. No specialist expertise or outside intervention is necessary.

4. Operates directly upon the target behaviour, and need not be concerned with long-term analysis of background features.

5. Procedure can be shared among a number of teachers, or between school and home.

Strategy :
1. Specify the behaviour, described in non-fuzzy terms, which is to be the target.

2. Define the behaviour in a clear and accurate way, i.e. that incidents can be observed and counted.

3. Decide on alternative and acceptable behaviours to replace the target behaviour.

4. Select a series of reinforcers -
   (a) Social
   (b) Tangible .....

that will be used consistently to follow the desired behaviour.

5. Decide on a method of recording and establish a baseline, e.g. the number of incidents of the target behaviour observed in a 1/2-hour period.

6. Initiate the programmes,
   (a) By praising the child for incidents of positive behaviour.
   (b) Ignoring incidents of target behaviour.
   (c) Providing tangible rewards (such as tokens) after each 1/2-hour period in which no incidents of target behaviour is observed.

A pre-decided number of tokens are to be exchanged for some tangible reward.

7. Recording is continued to determine if positive change is happening, with the child taking part in the recording process. If progress is poor or variable, one should check if the behaviour is being reinforced consistently; if the reinforcer is sufficient; or if unwitting attention to the target behaviour is being provided (including by peers).

8. With time, and improvement, one can gradually "fade" the reinforcement. Behaviours, once learned, are best maintained by occasional, even rare, reinforcement.

Research :
Much evidence exists for the effectiveness of this kind of approach to tackle a range of types of behavioural difficulty. The effectiveness of contingent teacher attention and praise was described in an early study of Barcroft (1970); and the rapid diminution of disruptive behaviour in a second year junior class was described by Appleton (1977).

References :
Barcroft, J. (1970) Behaviour Modification in the School.
M. Phil. Thesis. University of London.

Appleton, C. (1977) A Technology of Contingency Management of Disruptive Behaviour.
British Association of Behavioural Psychotherapy. Bulletin 5. 1. 7-51 .

Activity : Self-Monitoring of Disruptive Behaviours

Purpose : Reducing the incidence of difficult and disruptive behaviour in a mainstream class.

Age Levels : Primary to early comprehensive age groups; approximately Year 4 to Year 8.

Benefits :
1. The "ownership" of the behaviour and the procedure is with the pupils.

2. Simplicity of procedure.

3. The emphasis upon pupil - rather than teacher recording is likely to have a greater motivating effect.

4. A number of children who display disruptive behaviour can be involved.

5. The procedure can be used by school staff and parents in partnership.

Strategy :
1. The teacher identifies one or more pupil(s) whose behaviour interferes with their own, and peers' learning.

2. These pupils are observed for a given time period (say 30 minutes) over several days to record the frequency of the target behaviour, such as ... leaving the desk; calling out; hitting, or interfering with others.

3. The teacher explains to the pupils that they will receive points according to a system:-
   (a) 5 points for fewer than 5 disruptive behaviours per period.
   (b) 3 points for fewer than 10.

N.B. "Period" may be the time between assembly and break; break and lunch time; lunch time to break; break to end of school-day. Alternatively, it may refer to chunks of the classroom day, such as 45 minute sessions.

4. The teacher discusses a "reward menu" with the pupils indicating for what the accumulated points may be exchanged.

Rewards may be tangible ... such as pencils or rubbers, etc. . or social ... such as choice of seat in class, a positive note to take home, etc. One might also allow rewards to be shared with the whole class, such as a free choice of activity.

5. The pupils record each incident of a disruptive behaviour on a simple chart.

6. Initially the teacher monitors behaviour as well, and rewards are given if the teacher and pupil records are in accord. If there is a wide discrepancy, the reward is not given. With time, recording is taken over solely by the pupil.

N.B.2
The procedure may become the more effective if parents take part in the process of reinforcing positive behaviour.

Research :
The general benefits of this procedure were described originally by Bolstad and Johnson (1972). Lovitt (1984) describes the success of the procedure in reducing disruptive behaviour in a mainstream class ... including the minimising of difficulties presented by pupils coming into the ordinary school from special schools or units

References :
Bolstad, O. and Johnson, S. (1972) Self-regulation of classroom.
Behaviour Journal of Applied Behaviour Analysis. 5. 455-465

Lovitt, T. (1984) Tactics for Teaching.
Columbus Ohio. Merrill Co.

Activity : Contingency Contracting at Home and School

Purpose : Reducing the incidence of inappropriate and disruptive behaviours of certain children.

Age Levels : Year 3 to Year 8 approximately.

Benefits :
1. Procedure may be implemented in the mainstream class and a number of children may be involved.

2. The pupil(s) can take a direct share in the setting up of the procedure, and can observe and monitor their own progress.

3 Procedure is based upon straightforward but well-established principles.

4. A range of different behaviours may be targeted; and the opportunity for teacher(s) and family to work together is afforded.

Strategy :
1. Having identified the child whose behaviour is causing concern one highlights those tasks which the child should complete (e.g. homework, class projects, etc.).

2. One records the activities or materials that the child likes (e.g. being outdoors, watching TV, etc.).

3. A 2-part contract is planned, Part 1 lists what is expected of the pupil plus the points to be gained; Part 2 is a list of the rewards and their cost in terms of points.

4. Contract is written with the pupil to whom the features are explained in more detail.

5. Parents are involved and given advice in respect of offering the child points for doing certain things at home (as listed in Parts 1 and 2 of the contract) and to record events.

6. Observe performance over a few days and modify the contract as appropriate, e.g. if certain tasks are still not done, such as homework, the points for such tasks can be increased, and fewer points allocated to other tasks for which there is less resistance.

Over a longer time-scale, certain tasks may be dropped from the contract if the child is observed to be completing them voluntarily and consistently .. alternatively, other behaviours may need to be added.

N.B.
 (a) The time-scale will depend upon the needs of the case and observed progress.
 (b) Pre-prepared recording sheets will aid the monitoring of behavioural rewards.

Research :
This procedure, and its effectiveness, was originally set out by Cantrell et. al. (1969), and there is much evidence from a range of sources to confirm the effectiveness of contracting (e.g. Rogers 1990).

References :
Cantrell, et. al. (1969) Contingency Contracting with School Problems.
Journal of Applied Behaviour Analysis. 2. 215-220.

Rogers, W. (1991) You Know the Fair Rule.
London, Longman.

ACTIVITY : "Time Out"

Purpose : A means of reducing the impact of disruptive behaviour on a peer group, and of gaining a period for reflection and planning.

Age Levels : All ages ... from Year 1 to Year 9/10.

Benefits :
1. A means of communicating that the behaviour is unacceptable and that other pupils' rights/needs must be safeguarded.

2. The procedure may be seen as part of the rules within the classroom, rather than as a punishment.

3. It provides a breathing space for pupil, class, and teacher; and encourages self-responsibility for behaviour.

Strategy :
There are three forms of time out: (a) instant; (b) delayed; (c) "preventive".

The first refers to action immediately contingent upon the behaviour; the second to a deliberate delay thus to ensure that the pupil does not learn how to avoid a particular demand; the third refers simply to seeking a reason to remove a child from a situation as a confrontation is brewing, e.g. to deliver a message.

1. Instant time out is adopted when the child in question is disrupting an activity, and when immediate action is necessary.

2. The child is directed to a "time out" corner or to a separate room which may be discreetly supervised by a member of staff.

3. The child is told in clear terms why this action has been taken and for how long s/he will remain apart from the group. (The behaviour, not the person, is emphasised.)

4. The time out place should be non-reinforcing such that there is no risk that, for example, unwitting attention makes time out attractive.

5. At the end of the agreed period, the child returns to the group. Positive behaviour is noted and reinforced. If the child is still unsettled the period is extended; and, in the case of older pupils, another adult (such as year leader or SEN co-ordinator) will plan the return to class with the pupil ... stressing the pupil's responsibility for monitoring/modifying behaviour.
   a) The use of time out should be part of a whole-school policy which is made known in advance to all members of the school community (including parents).
   b) The precise form and timing of this procedure may vary according to circumstances, child's age, etc. Thus, the above procedure is intended as a basic guide, but more specific planning might usefully be arranged as a result of in-school discussion involving senior staff, including the school's educational psychologist.

Research :
Time out may already be a well known procedure in many schools. What matters, according to various authors (e.g. Glasser 1986, or Rogers 1991) is:
 (a) That the procedure is a well established in school, practical and part of a sequence of action steps.
 (b) That the procedure is applied consistently.
 (c) That the time out period must be less desirable than the activity from which the child is removed.
Given this, the procedure can be effective in reducing problem behaviours.

References :
Glasser, W. (1986) Control Theory in the Classroom.
New York. Harper & Row.

Rogers, W. (1991) You Know the Fair Rule.
London. Longman.

Activity : Ignoring

Purpose : Reducing incidence of (minor) disruptive behaviour in the classroom.

Age Levels: Any age ... but particularly applicable to the primary age range, say Year 1/2 to Year 7/8.

Benefits :
1. Simplicity of procedure.

2. Utilises the very powerful effect of teacher attention/non-attention, and/or of peer attention/non-attention.

3. There is no specialist intervention necessary; the procedure, instead, is largely a systematic version of "routine" teacher style.

Strategy :
1. The teacher identifies clearly the behaviour(s) that are to be modified, and defines such behaviour in objective and "non-fuzzy" terms. These "target" behaviours are shared with the class, and alternative positive behaviours are similarly identified.

2. The target behaviour is ignored consistently. Further, all unwitting attention to the behaviour must be avoided ... i.e. a glance, a raising of eyebrows, etc.

3. All examples of incompatibly desirable behaviour are praised.

4. It is likely that, initially, the target behaviour will increase in frequency or intensity (representing the child's heightened efforts to gain attention). Continuing to ignore totally the target behaviour is critical at this point.

N.B.
  (a) Ignoring a behaviour will not bring about an immediate change ... a significant period of time must be allowed for the strategy to work.
  (b) It is important to ensure that the target behaviour is not wittingly or unwittingly reinforced by attention from other pupils. It may be appropriate to offer social or tangible rewards to the whole class for their pointed ignoring of target behaviour.
  (c) "Ignoring" may not be the appropriate strategy for serious misbehaviour, but fits target behaviour which represents a minor irritant, and which, if reinforced by attention, would threaten the learning atmosphere.

Research :
Tanner (1978) stresses how systematic ignoring can be highly effective in reducing certain behaviours; and O'Leary and O'Leary (1977) cite evidence for the reduction of negative behaviours as a result of ignoring by looking away and remaining silent.

References :
Tanner, L. (1978). Classroom Discipline. Holt.

O'Leary, D. and O'Leary, S. (1977) Classroom Management.
Pergamon Press.

Activity : "Stop: Look: Listen: Think" (A form of cognitive behaviour therapy.)

Purpose : Reducing incidence of disruptive behaviour and controlling hyperactivity by self-management.

Age Levels : First and Middle age groups from year 2/3 to year 6/7 approximately.

Benefits :
1. The avoidance of labelling the child thus reducing any risk of lowered expectations and negative self-fulfilling prophecies.

2. Simplicity of procedure, involving no "external" intervention, and, thus, minimal threat to child's self-image or self-esteem.

3. Child remains fully part of the mainstream group, and the procedure is relatively "covert".

Strategy :
The procedure is based on the 3 stages of initiating/inhibiting behaviour proposed by Luria (1966),
   (a) Child's behaviour is controlled and directed by the speech of others.
   (b) Child begins to use overt speech to regulate own behaviour.
   (c) Inner speech takes over the regulatory role.

1. Child is observed to confirm the stage s/he is at.

2. "Helper" (teacher, or assistant) highlights with the child those aspects of behaviour which are disruptive to his/her progress and to the class

3. "Helper" arranges some signal to indicate to the child that a given behaviour is becoming a problem. Child is encouraged to talk over the actions, highlighting the negative effects.

4. On receipt of subsequent "signals", the child is to talk himself/herself through the actions thus to ensure awareness of what s/he is doing and the likely effects of the behaviour.

5. When the "signal" is given, the child talks internally over what is happening and reminds himself/herself about what is the unwanted behaviour and what is the preferred behaviour.

6. The "signals" are gradually faded out.

N.B.
   (a) There is a need for a high level of praise or positive reinforcement for those occasions where the child is showing good performance and avoiding difficult behaviour.
   (b) The benefits may be more rapid or greater if the initial helper-child discussions are held during brief individual sessions, and are followed up by brief sessions devoted to offering praise.
   (c) Reinforcement may be more effective if followed up by the parents and if shared by peers.

Research :
Benefits in respect of reducing disruptive behaviour and helping children to take control of their own behaviours are described by Ross and Ross (1976).

References:
Luria, A. (1966) Human Brain and Psychological Processes.
London. Harper and Row.

Ross, D. and Ross, S. (1976) Hyperactivity Research.
Chichester. Wiley.

Activity : "Neuro-Linguistic" Spelling Strategy

Purpose : Enhancing spelling through a visual approach.

Age Levels : Year 2/3 to adult.

Benefits :
1. Provision of an alternative to a phonic approach .... especially useful in dealing with irregular words.

2. Enhances the visual imagery for words and removes reliance on rote memory.

3. Enhances proof-reading and an awareness of when a word "looks right".

Strategy :
1. The student is encouraged to think of a situation or setting or object that is pleasant and familiar. When a positive and relaxed feeling has been gained, the student looks at the target word for 10 seconds. Ideally the word is in the upper left part of the visual field.

2. The student looks away from the word, and moves his/her eyes up and to the left, while trying to remember the correct spelling of the word. Any gaps are noted, and the student looks back at the word to check the letters.

3. This process is repeated until the word can be pictured in full and correctly.

4. The student looks up at the mental image and writes down the word from the mental model. The word is checked against the original written model. If the spelling is not correct the student returns to step 1.

5. The student looks again at the mental image and spells the word backwards ... thus to ensure that the image is really clear.

N.B. It may be helpful if:
  a) The word is visualised in the student's favourite colour.
  b) Parts of the word that prove difficult may be made to stand out in the visual image, i.e. bigger, different colour, etc.
  c) Longer words may be broken into chunks of 3-4 letters, albeit sufficiently small that the whole word can be seen. The letters may be traced in the air, or on the arm.

Research :
The benefits of this approach were set out by Dilts (1983); and positive results from tests of the strategy were quoted by O'Connor and Seymour (1990).

References :
Dilts, R. (1983) Applications of Neuro-Linguistic Programming.
California. Meta Publications.

O'Connor, J. and Seymour, J. (1990). Introducing Neuro Linguistic Programming.
London. Crucible Books.

Activity : Simultaneous Oral Spelling

Purpose : Enhancing accuracy and fluency of spelling.

Age Levels : Largely primary level (i.e. year 2/3 - year 6) but may also apply to older pupils.

Benefits :
1. Simplicity of procedure.

2. Procedure can be implemented by class teacher, support teacher, ancillary, parent or older pupil; and may be used at home or at school.

3. Proven effectiveness despite low time commitment.

4. Target words are selected by or for the pupil to fit his/her level and the context.

5. Evidence demonstrates that there is good generalisation from one set of words to another; and the method appears equally beneficial to a range of types of literacy difficulty, whether specific or more generalised.

Strategy :
1. The pupil indicates a word that s/he wants to learn.

2. The word is written down clearly, or made with plastic letters, for the pupil.

3. The pupil names the word.

4. The pupil writes the word, saying the name of each letter as it is written.

5. The pupil says the word again and checks that it has been copied correctly.

Steps 2 - 5 are repeated and the model word is covered as soon as the pupil feels confident that it is not required.

6. The pupil practises words over a period of 6 consecutive days.

7. The pupil is encouraged to generalise from a target word to words with similar sounds or orthographic patterns, using plastic letters.

Research :
Bradley and Bryant (1985) describe the success in terms of generalising from one word to another; and claim that the whole procedure requires only 30 seconds per word and that it is effective for pupils at all levels of literacy, from non-readers to college students. Bradley (1981) suggests that this technique is effective because it promotes the organisation of the correct writing pattern; and other authors (e.g. Thomson 1984) highlight the efficacy of the multi-sensory elements ... auditory, visual, motor and tactile.

References :
Bradley, L. and Bryant, P. (1985) Rhyme and Reason in Reading and Spelling.
University of Michigan Press.

Bradley, L. (1981) The organisation of motor patterns for spelling.
Developmental Medicine and Child Neurology 23. 83-91.

Thomson, M. (1984) Developmental Dyslexia.
London. Whurr Publishers.

Activity : Initial Spelling Teaching and Individualised Spelling Assignments

Purpose : Enhancing accuracy of spelling and establishing a spelling routine.

Age Levels : Year 2/3 to Year 6/7.

Benefits :

1. Individualised programmes which can be part of the classroom routine.

2. Minimising a child's anxiety over failure and increasing willingness to try difficult words.

3. The linking of spelling with "free" writing, thus highlighting the purpose of accurate spelling.

4. The establishment of good practice.

Strategy :
1. Child encouraged to write freely. Where s/he does not ask for any unfamiliar words but has a try at them and asterisks those where there is some uncertainty whether they are correct. (This provides further diagnostic material for the teacher in determining those words which the child clearly does not know, as well as errors which s/he does not recognise.)

2. Child reads work with the teacher (or adult helper) and together, they identify some of the mis-spellings, emphasising high frequency words.

3. The child writes the words to be learnt in her own notebook.

4. Words are to be learnt one at a time by the visual technique... Look-Say-Trace-Cover-Write-Check. The child can self-check by means of having target words written on a folded sheet of paper, or in a book with masking sheets.

5. Child is shown other words in the "visual family" and highlights the particular sequence of letters causing difficulty.

6. When the word is correctly spelt on 2 consecutive occasions in the Look-Say-Trace-Cover-Write-Check system, the child is encouraged to write a sentence containing the word.

7. Children can check their own progress by testing each other in pairs, and can set their own targets for the number of words to be learnt in a week.

N.B. Spelling progress will be accelerated if:
  (a) One talks with the child about how the word is made up.
  (b) The child is encouraged to "see" the word with eyes closed, not "sounded" letter by letter.
  (c) Words are practised from memory, not copied (i.e. asked-for words are written for the child, but
      removed before s/he writes).
  (d) Praise and positive feedback are maximised.

Research :
The general principles set out are based on long term observation and described by Peters and Cripps (1978).

Further, converging evidence emphasises the importance of ensuring the use of writing and spelling as opposed to highlighting narrow sub-skills (e.g. Reason et. al. 1988).

References :
Peters, M. and Cripps, C. (1978) Catchwords - Ideas for Teaching Spelling.
London. Harcourt, Brace, Jovanovich.

Reason, R., Brown, B., Cole, M. and Gregory, M. (1988) Does the "specific" in SpLD make a difference to the way we teach?
Support for Learning 3. 4. 230-236.

Activity : Cued Spelling

Purpose : Increasing accuracy and fluency of spelling.

Age Levels : Year 3 to Years 8/9

Benefits :
1. Simplicity of procedure.

2. For use with any number of children.

3. May be used at home as well as at school.

4. Ownership of procedure shared by teacher and pupils.

5. Time commitment is minimal such that classroom routines are not interrupted.

Strategy :
1. The child with spelling weakness is paired with a tutor (peer or parent).

2. The child selects "target" words to be learnt (either relating to individual choice or to relevance for current topics).

3. The child and partner check the spelling of a given word and the correct version is written into the Cued Spelling book.

4. The child reads the word with the partner, then alone to ensure that the word is read/articulated accurately.

5. Cues (prompts or reminders) are chosen to aid memory for the written word. These cues may be phonic sounds, or word patterns, or any device, with the proviso that the selection is made by the child. Child and partner say the cues together.

6. The child says the cues, and the partner writes the word.

7. The partner says the cues. and the child writes the word.

8. Child says cues and writes word.

9. Child writes the word and reads it. (If errors are noted at step 7 or 8, return to the step before.)

N.B. Each day the child writes all the words learnt that day. For a wrong word, the learning steps are repeated.

Each week the "mastery review" involves the child's writing all words learnt during that week. Wrong words may be added to the list of target words of the next week.

Research :
Watt and Topping (1993) describe a project of cued-spelling in a primary school. An average of 12 words were learnt each week, with parents or peers acting as tutors. Over a 4 month period, the mean gain in spelling age was 10 months for the parent-tutor group and 5.2 months for the peer-tutor group. Self-correction generalised to other settings and self-confidence was enhanced.

References :
Watt, J. and Topping, K. (1993) Cued Spelling.
Educational Psychology in Practice. 9.2. 95-103.

Further research demonstrating positive outcomes :

Emerson, P. (1988) Parent tutored cued spelling in a primary school.
Paired Reading Bulletin. 4. 91-92.

Brierley, M. et. al. (1989) Reciprocal peer tutored cued spelling with 10 year olds.
Paired Learning 5. 136-140

Activity : Word Families (Phonological Awareness)

Purpose : Fostering awareness of sounds in words, and the making of generalisations about spelling.

Age Levels : First school pupils.

Benefits :

1. The enhancing of attention to particular visual patterns of letters within words.

2. The linking of visual with auditory input.

3. Allows for the fact that children with developing reading retardation may be a diverse group who set about reading in a range of ways.

4. Emphasises the connection between reading and spelling.

5. Simplicity of approach which can be used in any setting.

Strategy :

1. Child selects a word.

2. "Helper" makes that word with plastic letters.

3. Child copies the model, then makes the word with plastic letters without the model.

4. Helper encourages the child to make further words by substituting the initial letter. These words are read to the helper, who draws attention to the common element of the words.

5. Gradually the word patterns become more complex.

   e.g. - at - eat - sh - ight, etc.

6. Words learnt can be rehearsed at intervals, and the child encouraged to use the words in simple written sentences.

Research :
Their approach, and its efficacy, are described by Bradley and Bryant (1985).

The value of the multi-sensory element is also underlined by Harding (1986).

References :
Bradley, L. and Bryant, P. (1985) Rhyme and Reason in Reading and Spelling.
University of Michigan Press.

Harding, L. (1986) Learning Disabilities in the Primary Classroom.
London. Croom-Helm.

Activity : Fernald Tracing (Look, Say, Do)

Purpose : Increasing reading competence by whole-word learning.

Age Levels : Year 1/2 - Year 3/4 (approximately) or older pupils with SpLD.

Benefits :
1. Provision of alternative approach to the child for whom a phonic method has minimal meaning.

2. Effective in teaching new words which are irregular, which need to be learnt quickly, or which are used frequently but present difficulties.

3. May be defined as a "multi-sensory" approach, and "meaning" is emphasised.

4. Procedure can be individualised to suit a child's level and the task context.

5. Procedure can be continued at home; and implemented by teacher, assistant, parent, sibling, or other pupil.

Strategy :
1. Word required is written for the child in large print on a standard sized strip of paper (2 x 12 inches).

2. Child traces over word with finger, saying each part aloud. This is repeated until the child can write and say the word without the model. The word must always be written as a whole; with errors or interruptions the child begins again.

3. When the word has been written correctly, the child incorporates it in a story or uses it to label a picture ... saying the word quietly while writing it.

4. As further words are learnt, the child may begin to make his/her own book about anything of interest (selecting words of direct relevance to the interests of the child is an important feature).

5. Whatever the child writes is typed or printed by the helper, and the child reads back the printed version the next day.

6. Words learnt are filed in alphabetic order. (The emphasis on initial letter is a positive basis for later dictionary work).

N.B. After an initial period, the tracing of words can be omitted, and the child encouraged to learn a new word simply by looking at it, saying it over, and writing it without looking at the copy while saying the word once again.

As vocabulary builds up, so "stories" become longer. The child should always read back what s/he has written, and the printed copy the next day.

After a further period still, the child is encouraged to learn directly from a printed word without it written separately on a strip of paper.

The significant feature is the link between the articulation of the word and the hand movement.

Research :
The efficacy of the method in developing vocabulary, enhancing confidence, and increasing motivation is described by Myers and Hammill (1976).

Hulme (1981) has also used the technique to demonstrate how the writing of a word is effective in identifying correct spelling patterns.

References :
Myers, P. and Hammill, D. (1976) Methods for Learning Disorders.
New York. Wiley.

Hulme, C. (1981) Reading Retardation and Multi-sensory Teaching.
London. Routledge.

Activity : "Coventry Technique"

Purpose : Teaching a basic sight vocabulary based on the child's own language.

Age Levels : Year 1/2 to Year 4 approximately, or beyond in the case of marked general or specific learning difficulties.

Benefits :
1. Individualisation of approach, using vocabulary according to the child's interests and choice.

2. Child's own natural language is used, such that meaning and purpose are highlighted.

3. High level of consolidation of material.

4. Simplicity of procedure that can be carried out in school or at home and implemented by teachers, assistants, parents or older pupils.

Strategy :
1. Prompted as necessary, the child chooses a topic for an interest book.

2. The child chooses a picture which is stuck into his/her book.

3. "Helper" and child discuss the picture to establish relevant vocabulary.

4. The child dictates a sentence to be written below the picture.

5. The child is encouraged to re-read the sentence, on successive occasions.

6. As the interest book progresses, the child returns to earlier pages to reinforce the material.

N.B. The procedure can be augmented by activities such as the following:
 (a) Matching separate sentence strips to those in the interest book.
 (b) Tracing over the "helper's" writing.
 (c) Copying the sentence with encouragement to write words from memory as far as possible.
 (d) Cutting up the sentence to show words and spaces, and rebuilding the sentence.
 (e) Storing words in a "Breakthrough" folder, on an alphabetic basis and using them to make further sentences/phrases.
 (f) Using the stored vocabulary to make "cloze" sentences with key words deleted.

Research :
This procedure was originally described by Brennan (1978), and follow-up work has been completed by Educational Psychologists (e.g. in the Coventry EPS) to demonstrate a positive effect upon progress and upon motivation.

Reference :
Brennan, W. (1978) Reading for Slow Learners.
Schools Council Curriculum. Bulletin 7. London. Methuen.

Activity : Pause, Prompt, Praise

Purpose : Enhancing accuracy and fluency of reading among slow readers.

Age Levels : Year 2 to Year 7/8.

Benefits :
1. Simplicity of procedure.

2. A structure for the hearing of reading in any setting.

3. Establishing of strategies leading to self-sufficiency.

4. Procedure can be implemented by any "helper" (teacher, parent, assistant, peer or sibling).

Strategy :
1. Child selects book from a range at instructional level.

2. Child encouraged to read aloud.

3. With an error or an omission, the helper pauses for 5 seconds to allow the child to self-correct, to recognise the error, or to produce the word.

4. If the child does not read the word correctly, the helper gives one or more prompts:
 (a) Reminder of picture cue.
 (b) Review of what went before.
 (c) Encouragement to look ahead.
 (d) Exploring the thinking behind the child's guess.
 (e) Reminder of a clue in the initial letter.
 (f) Encouragement to use phonic cues ... blends, endings, etc.
If the child does not read the word after 2 or 3 prompts, the helper gives the word and the child continues reading .

N.B.
1. All attempts at self-correction are praised.

2. The praise is specific, e.g. Comment on the use of context. Praise for listening to what is read for the child.

3. Opportunities are taken to discuss the parts of words that give cues, to practise sound-blending, and to practise earlier words that presented difficulty.

Research :
The effectiveness of the technique is highlighted by Wheldall et al (1987) who describe how praising successful strategies will establish the routine of using those strategies when the child is reading alone, and lead to greater independence.

References :
Wheldall, K., Merrett, F. and Colmas, S. (1987) Pause, prompt and praise for parents and peers: effective tutoring of low progress readers.
Support for Learning. 21. 5-12.

Activity : Language Experience Approach

Purpose : Enhancing the confidence and literacy competence of young children.

Age Levels : Primary age range (Year 2 to Year 6/7 approximately) or older children with marked literacy difficulties.

Benefits :

1. The easy prediction, on the part of the child, of the text.

2. Access to written form of words commonly used, and thus, enhanced visual-recognition skills.

3. The promotion of free writing.

4. Enhanced awareness of the purpose of written language in communicating ideas or information.

5. Enhanced positive self-image as a writer and reader.

6. Maximal individualisation of the material.

7. Approach may be used at school or at home, involving teacher, parent, assistant, voluntary helper or older pupil.

Strategy :

1. The child composes. orally, a short story; or an account of some event or experience.

2. The story is written by the "helper" exactly as it was told.

3. Helper re-reads the text to the child to see if any changes are to be made.

4. Story is then re-written in a neat form (or ideally, typed or printed).

5. The story then becomes the child's own reading material to be read to the helper, other adults, or peers.

6. Each story is added to the child's own book, to which s/he is encouraged to add illustrations.

7. Helper may select certain words to practise, or to use as a basis for "word-family" work; and, as the child's confidence grows, indicate a small number of words whose spelling can be corrected.

8. With time, the child can be asked to write his/her stories. Even very poor spellers will be able to remember the content such that;
   (a) The child can enjoy the process of communicating and using literacy.
   (b) The helper can select certain words to practise ... albeit ensuring that emphasis on neatness and spelling does not stifle the willingness to express ideas.

Research :
Goulandris (1985) highlights the value of the Language experience approach in enhancing pupil confidence to write, developing sight vocabulary, and providing a structure for specific teaching of given words or word patterns.

Harding (1986) describes the efficacy of the approach in terms of gaining awareness of the use of literacy and of the language of books, thus ensuring access to "real" reading.

References :
Goulandris, N. (1985) Extending the written language skills of children with specific learning difficulties. In Snowling, (ed.) Children's Written Language Difficulties.
Windsor. NFER-Nelson.

Harding, L. (1986) Learning Disabilities in the Primary Classroom.
London. Croom-Helm.

Activity : Visuo-thematic Approach (a variant of the Language Experience Approach)

Purpose : Developing sight vocabulary and enhancing fluency in "real" reading.

Age Levels: : Primary level (or older in the case of marked general or specific learning difficulty).

Benefits :
1. Rapid growth in word recognition repertoire.

2. Simplicity of procedure that can be used in any setting.

3. Individualisation of the material to suit the child and his interests.

4. Demonstrates the purpose of literacy and provides the experience of communicating ideas.

5. Provision of a structure within which to record and practise vocabulary, and to explain word-attack skills (by focusing on particular blends or letter-strings).

Strategy :
1. Child is presented with (or chooses) a stimulus picture.

2. Picture is discussed by the child and helper, who may furnish occasional prompts, thus to generate a simple story.

3. A sheet of paper is used, ruled into 3 columns headed: naming words; describing words; action words.

Child is asked to think of as many words as possible for each column, and these are written in by the helper (teacher, or parent, or assistant).

4. Child or helper writes the words, while saying them on separate pieces of paper which are placed in a box or envelope ... thus building a "library" of vocabulary ... and the picture is attached to the box/envelope.

5. At the next session, the helper checks the child's accuracy in saying the words when presented with the written words and the child practises writing the words.

6. Child is encouraged to write a story about the picture and give it a title. Child reads the story with the helper and any inaccuracies are corrected.

7. Child re-writes (or types/prints) the story, and sticks it into a book.

8. Such a sequence is implemented once or twice per week, and the various stories (or separate words) are practised at the start of each subsequent session.

Research :
The success of this approach in building confidence in previously reluctant or disabled readers, and in accelerating progress, is set out by Jackson (1972); and is highlighted as an effective yet simple procedure by Westwood (1987).

References :
Jackson, M. (1972) Reading Disability. Experiment, Innovation and Individual Therapy.
Sydney. Angus & Robertson.

Westwood, P. (1987) Common-sense Methods for Children with Special Needs.
London. Routledge.

Activity : Cloze Procedure

Purpose : Increasing the motivation for, and the accuracy of, reading in pupils with reading retardation or with limited comprehension/memory of content.

Age Levels : Largely primary age levels. Year 3 - Year 7/8 approximately.

Benefits :

1. The match between spoken and written language, with the probability of enhanced motivation for reading tasks.

2. An example of "real" reading.

3. Procedure lends itself to small group working with implications for social and (expressive) language development, as well as for literacy.

4. A means of ensuring attention to syntactic as well as to semantic cues for word recognition, and a balance to a phonic decoding approach.

Strategy :

1. Child dictates or writes a story (with a length between 100 and 150 words).

2. Story is typed or printed, and a "cloze" version is prepared where certain words are omitted. This may be done in a number of ways:
   (a) Deleting all structural words like "for, in, with, after, etc."
   (b) Deleting all nouns.
   (c) Deleting all action verbs.
   (d) Deleting all adverbs/adjectives.
   (e) Deleting every 'n'th word.
   (f) Deleting according to position in sentence.

The methods will vary according to the child's needs/abilities.

3. Child is told the kind of words omitted, and is asked to read the passage and fill in the missing words.

4. The child's version is compared to the original version with a view to highlighting:
   (a) Visual or other cues that aid word recognition.
   (b) How "wrong" insertions may change the meaning of the passage.

Where appropriate, the child may be given additional information to aid the process of selecting the missing words. For example, the initial letters may be supplied, or the number of letters may be indicated by dots, or the shape of the missing word may be outlined.

Research :
The effectiveness of the approach in accelerating reading progress among pupils of a range of ability has been described by Rye (1982) who emphasises the importance of discussion of the choice of words.

References :
Rye, J. (1982) Cloze Procedure and the Teaching of Reading.
London. Heinemann.

Activity : A.R.R.O.W. Technique

Purpose : Enhancing accuracy and fluency of reading and spelling and enhancing receptive and expressive language.

Age Levels : Primary age pupils (Year 2 to Year 6 approximately).

Benefits :
1. Use of technique is rapidly learned by the pupil.

2. The recording of the pupil's own voice enhances motivation and increases the efficacy of the time spent on this technique.

3. Pupil can work largely independently, and the difficulties are not made evident to peers.

4. Consequent material can be individualised to suit a given pupil's level and choice of material.

Strategy:
1. Pupil is provided with a tape recorder (ideally a 2-track machine) and headset, including headphones and microphone.

2. Aural: The pupil listens to a reading of words or a passage, pre-recorded by teacher, parent, assistant or volunteer helper.

3. Read: The pupil follows the written words or text as s/he listens. (With non-readers, visual support material can be provided.)

4. Respond: Following the simultaneous listening and following of the words, the pupil is encouraged to imitate the words given on the tape.

5. Oral: The pupil repeats the pre-recorded words and listens to a replay of his or her own recorded speech. When this has been done the adult's voice can be switched off, and the pupil follows the written words while listening to his own recording of those words.

6. Written: While listening to a replay of her own voice, the pupil is encouraged to write down the words. (Non-readers may be asked to arrange visual materials in a sequence matching the recorded material.)

Research :
Goulandris (1985) describes the value of using this recording technique as an aid to memorising. It is also noted that listening to their own voices is more effective for children than listening to recordings made by others.

Lane (1990) reports the effectiveness of the ARROW approach in improving children's language abilities, both receptive and expressive; and in enhancing listening skills, short-term memory, reading accuracy, comprehension and spelling.

References :
Goulandris, N. (1985) Extending the Written Language Skills of Children with Specific Learning Difficulties.
In Snowling (ed.) Children's Written Language Difficulties.
Windsor. NFER-Nelson.

Lane, C. (1990) ARROW: alleviating children's reading and spelling difficulties.
In Pumfrey and Elliott (eds.) Children's Difficulties in Reading, Spelling and Writing.
London. Falmer Press.

Activity : Precision Teaching

Purpose : Assessing the best method of teaching basic skills and thus, accelerating skill acquisition.

Age Levels: : Principally the primary age range, but the technique may be applied to older pupils and students.

Benefits :
1. Provision for the teacher of a systematic means of evaluating a teaching programme, and of demonstrating if teaching should be modified.

2. Teacher remains free to select from a range of interventions including the more traditional approaches.

3. A number of children can be helped with this technique without any loss of contact with class routines.

4. The technique can be shared with parents and practised at home as well as at school; or may be implemented by support staff in the school.

5. Efficient form of record-keeping, and of establishing objectives.

6. Rapid daily feedback for both teacher and pupil.

7. Economic use of direct teaching and assessment time.

Strategy :
1. A child is targeted by classroom observation of slow progress in basic educational skills, and a given area is selected for attention, e.g. sight vocabulary.

2. The desired pupil performance is specified in observable and measurable terms, e.g. "John will read, with no errors, the 10 key words, selected by his teacher from the current reading book, when presented on flashcards".

3. Each day, a brief period is set aside for teaching to the specified skills, and the performance is recorded, and charted on the appropriate forms.

4. The performance is analysed to determine whether progress is satisfactory or unsatisfactory. If the latter, changes in teaching approach are considered thus to maintain or accelerate progress.

Research :
Benefits in terms of accelerated progress, parental involvement and pupil confidence are summarised by Raybould (1981), and Lovitt and Haring et al (1979).

References :
Raybould, E. (1981) Precision Teaching. in Wheldall, K. (ed.). The Behaviourist in the Classroom. Educational Review Publications. Birmingham University.

Lovitt, T. and Haring, N, (1979) Classroom Application of Precision Teaching. Washington, Seattle. Special Child Publications.

N.B.
1. "Data-Pac" is a form of Precision Teaching where there is a ready-prepared resource bank of teaching objectives plus materials to work on reading, spelling, numeracy and handwriting.

2. The school's educational psychologist would offer further advice on the implementation of the Precision Approach.

3. Please see "Precision Teaching", the Descriptive Summary produced by Connor M.J. (1991), available via the Surrey EPS.

Activity : Proof-Reading

Purpose : Increasing spelling accuracy.

Age Levels : Year 3 and above.

Benefits :
1. Establishing a routine of self-checking and, thus, good practice.

2. Enhancing attention to grapheme patterns.

3. Individualisation of the strategy.

4. Ownership of the strategy is largely with the child.

5. Expression of ideas is not inhibited.

Strategy :
1. In a piece of the pupil's free writing, the teacher underlines those spelling errors that the pupil is likely to be able to correct for him/herself.

2. Pupil makes the appropriate corrections.

3. Pupil encouraged, on completion of next piece of writing, to underline dubious spellings.

4. Pupil given help, where appropriate, on the use of a dictionary:
   (a) Introducing dictionary "quartiles" A-D, E-M, N-R, S-Z.
   (b) Providing practice in locating words, in these quartiles, by initial letter.
   (c) Providing practice in locating words with particular blends or combinations of letters at their beginning.

5. Self-correcting of free writing, and listing of words which gave difficulty in an individual spelling dictionary.

6. Random selection of words listed to be practised either at home or at school on a weekly basis.

7. Finally, the pupil is encouraged to question spelling as s/he writes, and not at the end of the piece of writing.

Research :
Persanke and Yee (1971) demonstrated how those boys who had been encouraged to proof-read, and who had been given practice in locating unfamiliar words in a dictionary, rapidly showed a decrease in spelling errors compared to controls not taught this technique.

References :
Persanke, C. and Yee, A. (1971) Comprehensive Spelling Introduction: Theory, Research and Application. Scranton International Textbook Co.

Activity : Peer Modelling of Behaviour

Purpose : The reduction of difficult and disruptive behaviour in the mainstream class.

Age Levels : Largely the mid-primary range ... say, Year 3 to Year 7/8.

Benefits :
1. A small group of children may be helped by this procedure, not just an individual.

2. The emphasis is placed upon desirable behaviour rather than on negative behaviour. There is a clear demonstration of what is acceptable behaviour.

3. The procedure is simple and involves no external or specialist intervention; and the "ownership" of the procedure and behaviour remains with the class.

Strategy :
1. The teacher identifies those pupils whose behaviour is having a disruptive effect, e.g. calling out, hitting other children, leaving their place, etc.

2. A similar number of pupils are identified as "models". These pupils are those perceived as socially mature and reliable.

3. The target pupils are told how and why their behaviour can sometimes be disruptive ... these behaviours are clearly spelled out to the pupils.

4. The models are invited to assist in modifying these behaviours and each model is paired with a target pupil, sitting next to each other. The model not only demonstrates appropriate behaviour but also reminds the partner when s/he is behaving inappropriately.

The target pupils are asked to watch their partners, and behave as they do and to ask them what to do if they are uncertain.

5. The models are asked also to offer praise when their partners work well.

N.B. The procedure could be used during the greater part of a school day, or may be limited to particular times or situations, e.g. school trips; practical activities.

Research :
The original work, described by Csapo (1972), demonstrated the effectiveness of using peers as models in reducing problem behaviour and in ensuring that the "target" children do know exactly what it is that they are supposed to do.

References :
Csapo, M. (1977) Peer models reverse the "one bad apple spoils the barrel" theory.
Teaching Exceptional Children. 5. 20-24.

Activity : Peer Management of Behaviour

Purpose : Reducing disruptive behaviour using peers as "therapists".

Age Levels : Primary age range ... Year 3 to Year 6.

Benefits :
1. Involves no external or specialist intervention.

2. The "ownership" of the behaviour and the procedure is with the pupils.

3. It reduces peer attention and re-enforcement towards problem behaviour and emphasises positive behaviour.

Strategy :
1. The pupils most frequently displaying disruptive behaviour are identified so that between 2 and 6 target pupils are selected.

2. A similar number of pupils are selected as therapists ... based upon observations of those who have the highest popularity and esteem.

3. The target behaviours are listed, e.g. being out of seat, talking, etc. Positive behaviours are also listed, e.g. working quietly on tasks, making positive contributions to class discussions, etc.

4. Having ensured that they wish to participate, the therapist pupils are taught to:
   (a) Point out to the target pupils the disruptive incidents, and praise the positive behaviours.
   (b) Generally to reinforce the good behaviour and to ignore the disruptive incidents.
   (c) Complete a score sheet on which target behaviours and positive behaviours are listed ... marking + or - as they respond to either type of behaviour.

5. The "therapist" pupils are paired with target pupils.

6. The procedure is monitored over the first day or two to ensure that the procedure is being followed and that the therapists are getting feedback/encouragement.

N.B.
   (a) The "therapists" could work together to help all the target pupils instead of working 1:1 .
   (b) The "therapists" might also assist in the identifying of target and positive behaviours.
   (c) The procedure could be applied during specific times, such as break or practical lessons, or throughout the day.

Research :
Lovitt (1984) notes that peers may be more skilled at pinpointing problems and solutions, and also emphasises that problems may be exacerbated by peer attention.

The original benefits of the procedure were set out by Solomon and Wahler (1973).

References :
Lovitt, T. (1984) Tactics for Teaching.
Ohio Merrill Publishing Co.

Solomon, R. and Wahler, R. (1973) Peer Reinforcement Control of Classroom Problem Behaviour.
Journal of Applied Behaviour Analysis. 6. 69-56.

Activity : The "Game Approach" to Classroom Management

Purpose : Reducing inattentive or disruptive behaviour.

Age Levels : Primary age range ... Year 2/3 to Year 7 approximately.

Benefits :
1. May be applied to a small group of children as much as to individuals.

2. Based on well tried principles which highlight the significance of peer attention as well as teacher attention.

3. Relative simplicity of procedure that can be implemented by the class teacher.

4. The procedure does not interfere with the teaching "style".

5. The procedure will highlight the behaviour that is wanted, rather than that which is not wanted.

Strategy :
1. The target behaviours are highlighted, and the corresponding preferred behaviours are listed, e.g. remaining in seats while working, allowing other children to work without interruption.

2. The "rules" are shared with the whole class, and are displayed in a prominent place in the classroom and the children's attention is drawn to them on regular occasions.

3. Use is made of a timer, such as a kitchen timer, or a cassette player prepared to sound a tone at variable intervals, on average, about 10-15 minutes apart (with a range of 5-25 minutes). The class is told that every time the tone is sounded, the teacher would look at one of the tables/groups and if the whole group was keeping the rules, then each child would receive a house point (or its equivalent). The order of looking at each table or group is random although everyone would have an equal number of turns.

4. When points are awarded, this is announced to the whole class by the teacher, accompanied by verbal praise.

5. With time, the reinforcement [the awarding of points] is reduced. The children are told that they can still gain points but not on every occasion; and the points are awarded with only 50% of the signals on a random basis ... although the verbal praise can still be offered consistently.

Research :
With a class of 10+ year old children, Merrett and Wheldall (1981) were able to demonstrate a significant increase in on-task behaviour and a reduction in disruptive behaviours. It was also found that the use of verbal reinforcers was very significant such that the effectiveness of the procedure would be enhanced if the teacher was able to rehearse the rules, frequently describe the benefits of keeping the rules, and maximise verbal/social reinforcement.

References :
Merrett, F. and Wheldall, K. (1981) A Game Approach to Behavioural Classroom Management in the Junior School. In Wheldall (ed.). Behaviours in the Classroom.
Offset Publications No. 1. University of Birmingham.

Activity : Social Skill Training

Purpose : Developing social/personal skills and enabling children to be accepted within peer groups.

Age Levels : Primary sector Year 3 to Year 6/7.

Benefits :

1. Reduction in the number of children with problems in interpersonal relations.

2. Reduction in the risk of the development of emotional/behavioural difficulties linked to social disadvantages.

3. Minimal use of specialist material.

4. An "active" programme involving learning through experience rather than instruction.

Strategy :

1. A "target" group of around 6 or 8 pupils is selected by means of class teacher observation, (an even number is appropriate to facilitate work with partners) and by clustering children with similar types of difficulty.

2. A programme of 6 hour-long sessions is set up noting that the precise content of the latter sessions may vary according to experience in the earlier sessions, e.g.
   (a) General introduction, including the showing of a video ("New Start" from the T.V. series "Talk, Write and Read") which concerns the first day at a new school. Discussion of content and of the difficulty in making friends; emphasis on conversation as a means of discovering shared interests. Children then hold 10-minute conversation in pairs in order to find out all about each other ... then feedback to the group.
   (b) Emphasis on communication as a 2-way process. Adult describes an interest and responds to questions. Following this model, children make their presentations and respond to questions. Final discussion covers activities which can be shared and of what spoils shared activities.
   (c) Children play a variety of board games in 2's and 3's.
   (d) Similar session ... but with no complication arising from unfamiliarity with the rules of the games.
   (e) Emphasis on co-operative play. Group is offered a set of construction materials and invited to choose something to build and build it together.
   (f) Further emphasis on co-operation with group invited to organise a party. Children to plan everything, such as games, food and drink, etc. Each child is allowed to invite one adult guest.

Research :

The above scheme, involving 8 pupils from Year 3 to Year 6, operated by Daniels (1990), brought about a number of positive changes, spontaneously described by the children themselves, viz. learning not to argue, learning to think about what others say, etc. Teacher comments indicated that only one child failed to benefit. All others were observed to relate to others more positively, with minimal instances of quarrelsome or spiteful behaviour, and to display enhanced confidence.

References :

Daniels, A. (1990) Social Skills Training for Primary Age Children.
Educational Psychology in Practice. 6. 3. 159-168.

N.B.
1. The time commitment is acknowledged, such that a programme of this kind may need to be implemented by the SEN co-ordinator or Support Teacher, or an adult other than class teacher (unless he/she can be freed for the weekly hour).

2. The above scheme is an illustration; precise content must be flexible and determined by experience and by the nature of the group in question. The "personalised" nature of any programme may lead to more positive outcomes than those linked to pre-arranged and published packages.

Activity : Coaching in Social Competence

Purpose : Enhancement of pupil's ability to interact co-operatively with others and the development of social skills.

Age Levels : First and Middle School levels ... say Year 2 to Year 6.

Benefits :

1. Social skills are encouraged within the "natural" setting of the classroom.

2. A range of appropriate group activities is available via published resource material.

3. Group size may be small or relatively large.

4. The procedure can be shortened if or when appropriate.

Strategy :

1. The teacher identifies a given social skill relevant to the child(ren) and introduces the skill by sharing ideas with the child(ren) about how games can be made more fun or how groups can work together more efficiently.

2. The teacher checks the understanding of the concept (e.g. co-operation) by asking for specific examples. The teacher rephrases the examples given or provides some examples.

3. The teacher asks for examples of behaviour that run counter to the concept: and then provides a number of types of behaviour, positive and negative, and asks the child(ren) to evaluate them, determining which will make a game more fun or a task easier to complete.

4. A particular game or activity is introduced and the teacher reminds the pupils of the positive examples of co-operation.

5. After the activity the child(ren) and teacher review the helpfulness of their examples and positive ideas are highlighted.

N.B.
Activities over and above the routine class tasks and games are listed in a number of publications such as:-

Social Skills in Interpersonal Communication. Hargie, et al . London. Routledge (1989).

Social Skill Training with Children and Adolescents. Spence, S. NFER-Nelson. (1985).

Coping with Conflict. Nicholas, F. LDA (1987).

Research :
Much evidence exists for the significance of social skill and social acceptance for well-being, adjustment, and scholastic achievement, e.g. Dunn & McGuire (1992).

The benefits of such an approach as that described above in terms of maximising social competence are set out by Oden (1980)

References :
Dunn, J. and McGuire, S. (1992). Sibling and Peer Relationships in Childhood.
Journal of Child Psychology and Psychiatry 33. 1. 67-105.

Oden, S. (1980) A Child's Social Isolation. in Cartledge and Milburn (eds.). Teaching Social Skills to Children. Pergamon Press.

Activity : Concept Circles

Purpose : Raising self-esteem and confidence.

Age Levels: : Younger primary range ...say year 1 to year 5.

Benefits :
1. Provision of insight for teachers into pupil concerns and feelings.

2. The activity can be arranged easily within the mainstream classroom, and involves no specialist intervention. The system is "owned" by the pupils and their teacher.

3. The enhancement of inter-pupil and pupil-teacher contact and relationship.

Strategy :
1. A group of children is organised to include those with observably low self-esteem or poor self-image. A group size between 12 and 20 appears the most appropriate.

2. The children are seated in a circle and the "rules" are shared, viz.:
   (a) Everyone remains seated in the same place.
   (b) Only positive (kind) comments are to be expressed.
   (c) Only one person speaks at a time. This is organised according to who is holding the token (a toy or a badge, etc.).

3. A number of topics may be utilised and these are selected by the teacher(s) who will be organising the group. Topics may include; "I am good at"; "The best thing about school is"; "I feel worried when", etc.

4. Once the particular topic is selected, the teacher (and any other adult in the circle) makes the initial contribution; and the topic is continued until all the children have had a turn.

N.B.
a) It may be useful to follow up the group discussion by setting down some of the content in writing to provide reading material for use in class, or to be shared with other adults, including parents.
b) "Magic Chair" is a variant of the procedure in that when a child sits in a particular place, it is the role of the other children to provide a positive comment about him/her.
c) The teacher, or other adult involved, may seek to reinforce particular comments and draw attention to certain positive aspects of behaviour described.
d) Some of the concerns expressed by the children may be followed up by actual changes in class or school routines.

Research :
This kind of approach may already be common practice in many schools, and the benefits in terms of pupil esteem and in-class relationships are described by Giddings & Page (1993).

Reference :
Giddings, S. and Page, T. (1993). Squaring the Circle.
Child Education. February. 48-49.

Activity : Friendship Groups

Purpose : The enhancement of social skills and of opportunities to integrate within a group.

Age Levels : Primary, and lower secondary, range, say Year 2 to Year 9.

Benefits :
1. Procedure is short-term and can be implemented within the mainstream class.

2. The relatively simple procedure can have a major impact upon social and personal adjustment (and, this, enhances intellectual and scholastic performance).

3. The procedure works in the "natural setting" of the school, and does not involve some external referral.

Strategy :
1. Teacher identifies the child or children who may be isolated, uninvolved with peers, or even subject to some teasing and overt rejection. This is largely a matter of observation of performance in class and during break times, plus discussion with other staff, supervisors, and parents.

2. To form a group, around 5 other children from the same class or year group are selected on the basis of their observed social maturity, approachability, etc. (and of their willingness to take part, plus parental permission).

3. The purpose of the group is set out to the participants, i.e. to underline the importance of having friends; to learn how to be and remain friends: and to discover how individuals differ ... and it is planned when and where to meet (weekly, for about 45 minutes in a room other than the classroom).

4. A range of activities is provided during the sessions which provides the opportunity, and need, for the group to share learning, planning, discussing, and co-operative working.

e.g. The "Broken Square" game where the group has to put together 4 or 5 pictures which have been cut into random pieces and muddled together.

(Other activities are listed in a range of sources, e.g. Spivack and Shure 1974, or Frederickson 1992).

5. After the activity discussion is led by the teacher (or assistant or SEN Co-ordinator, or whoever leads the group) in respect of what happened, what was the hard part, who did all the work, etc.

6. The leader offers feedback in terms of what was observed to be happening and invites the group to comment on how things had gone, and how they may have been improved.

Research :
The implementation of such a scheme, described by Rosenthal (1993), was found to lead to more positive demeanour among the target children, more incidence of co-operation in class, upturn in academic progress and greater social contact ... although it was not clear whether these positive changes would be maintained in the long term.

References :
Spivack, G. and Shure, M. (1974) Social Adjustment of Young Children.
San Francisco. Jossey.

Frederickson, N. (1992) Children can be so cruel.
Psychological Services for Primary Schools. London. Longman.

Rosenthal, H. (1993) Friendship Groups.
Educational Psychology in Practice. 9. 2. 112-120.

Activity : Welfare Support Groups

Purpose : Minimising disruptive behaviour and facilitating social skills.

Age Levels : Middle and Lower Comprehensive School pupils ... Year 3/4 to Year 9/10.

Benefits :
1. Ownership of behaviour is with the pupils, albeit aided by teachers and peers.

2. Facilitates a partnership of teacher, pupils, and parents.

3. Highlights the seriousness of the concern, but sets a positive atmosphere and expectation.

Strategies :
1. Where a pupil's behaviour is causing concern and has not responded to "routine" discipline, the parent(s) are invited to the school to work with the teacher and the pupil him/herself, to agree on a solution acceptable to all involved .

2. The meeting is convened to involve parents, teacher, year leader, pupil (and, if appropriate, parental advocate, or EP). Year leader to chair.

3. The conduct of the meeting is in the following stages:
   (a) Ice-breaking designed to stress that the purpose of the meeting is to define the problem and reach a plan of action.
   (b) All parties are invited to express their view of events (and "personal" comments or complaints are avoided in favour of a straightforward defining of the problem from an individual's perspective).
   (c) Each person generates possible solutions. Chairperson's role is crucial in listening to all views without appearing negative or judgmental, and in clarifying the precise nature of the problem.
   (d) The Chairperson leads the discussion towards highlighting the solution that will work out best for everyone. It is stressed that everyone has shared in the planning and that everyone is expected to maintain his/her part of the plan.
   (e) The agreed solution is restated clearly, and may be written. Ideally, the time scale should be fairly short to ensure some rapid success for pupil, teacher and parent.

4. The solution is tried for a given period, and the support group meets again to review progress. If problems are not diminishing, steps 3a - 3e are repeated. It is appropriate to avoid giving up the efforts too quickly if suspension or special provision would then follow.

Research :
The above procedure is set out by Rogers (1991) based upon experience as a teacher and consultant, including direct involvement with teachers seeking support in matters of discipline and class management.

Reference :
Rogers, W. (1991) You Know the Fair Rule.
London. Longman.

Activity : Reciprocal Teaching

Purpose : Assisting pupils to understand and to remember what they read.

Age Levels : Year 3/4 to Year 9 approximately.

Benefits :
1. The emphasis is placed upon enhancing pupils' responsibility for their own learning ... pupils act as teachers to small groups of peers ... such that self-sufficiency is enhanced.

2. Pupils are actively involved in learning with positive implications for motivation and memory.

3. The teacher's commitment to the procedure can gradually be reduced as the pupils become increasingly self-sufficient and able to stay on task.

Strategy :
1. A small group (4-5) of pupils is identified as having difficulty with the memory/comprehension of reading matter, even if decoding appears adequate.

2. Prior to reading a passage of text, the group discusses the title and sub-headings to "tune in" to background knowledge.

3. The teacher sets a series of questions or tasks to encourage pupils to...
   (a) Summarise what has happened so far.
   (b) Predict what is likely to happen, or what information is likely to be found, in the passage to be read.
   (c) Identify and rehearse difficult, unusual, or technical words in the passage.
   (d) Seek answers in the passage to a specific question posed.

4. The passage is read silently by members of the group, and the teacher leads discussion in respect of the content its significance and any difficult vocabulary.

5. Once the pattern is clear, the teacher role is taken over by one of the group and s/he takes the group through tasks (a)-(d).

The teacher role is passed around the group members in turn (thus involving the reciprocal element).

The teacher may increasingly withdraw from the group(s) and act simply as a monitor.

Research :
Further details, together with a description of the powerful benefits that transfer and generalise, are to be found in Moore (1988).

Reference :
Moore, P. (1988) Reciprocal Teaching and Reading Comprehension.
Journal of Research in Reading. 11. 1. 3-14.

Activity : Directed Activities Related to Texts (DARTS)

Purpose : Enhancing the meaningfulness of reading through heightened awareness of language patterns (semantic and syntactic).

Age Levels : Year 2 to year 7/8 approximately.

Benefits :
1. The small group provision will have benefits for social, language, and cognitive development.

2. There is an emphasis upon meaning and context, such that oral and written language are linked.

3. The level of task difficulty can readily be modified.

Strategy :
1. Small group of children is organised according to level of reading performance.

2. 3 basic tasks are organised by the "helper" (teacher or assistant):
   (a) Group Cloze: a passage with words deleted is presented and the children are invited to supply the words. This involves discussion of alternatives and re-reading of the text.
   (b) Group Sequencing: children are presented with the parts of a continuous sequence, such as cartoon pictures with or without "bubble" speech. Their task is to order the material and justify the sequence made.
   (c) Group Prediction: presented with the first part of a story, children are asked questions like "what is happening?", "What led to this?", "What will happen next?", etc. The children justify their suggestions by reference to the material and inter-group discussion is encouraged.

The material may be pictures only, pictures with bubble text or text only.

Research :
Pumfrey (1990) describes how the procedures may be used effectively with children of a range of abilities.

Beard (1987) describes how the procedures can capitalise on the children's oral language development, and the negotiation of meanings or predictions has a direct and positive impact on reading.

References :
Pumfrey, P. (1990) Testing and Teaching Pupils, in Pumfrey and Elliott (eds.) Children's Difficulties in Reading, Spelling and Writing.
London. Falmer Press.

Beard, R. (1987) Developing Reading 3-13.
London. Hodder and Stoughton.

Activity : Shared Writing

Purpose : Enhancing writing content, and confidence in writing, by collaboration with teacher and peers.

Age Levels : First school pupils (Year 1 to Year 2/3) or older pupils (up to year 4/5) with learning difficulty.

Benefits :
1. Children rapidly perceive the purpose of writing.

2. A model is provided of what writers do.

3. Provision of context where all children may feel free to contribute.

4. Writing is perceived as an enjoyable and meaningful activity.

5. Expression of ideas is facilitated.

6. Provides opportunity for teachers to observe the strengths or problems of individuals; and to draw attention to details of transcription.

Strategy :
1. A sub-group of children is established, ideally around 8, but no fewer than 4 or more than 15.

2. It is planned whether the group will re-tell a story, extend or make its own version of a story, or record some experience or event (i.e. the children will be familiar with the "raw material").

3. The teacher acts as a scribe using large sheets of paper which can be seen clearly by all the children. The teacher talks to the children to establish what the story is to be about (the characters and events).

4. Following questions to elicit initial ideas ("How shall we begin", etc.) the story is written down. Different children may contribute different ideas, and discussion is held to determine why a suggestion is or is not to be incorporated (with the teacher contributing as little as possible to the discussion).

5. While writing, the teacher can focus upon relevant transcriptional details such as ensuring spaces between words, the use of a full stop, certain spelling patterns, etc.

6. As the story continues, it is read frequently with the children suggesting what should be changed or what added ... thus highlighting that correcting is quite normal, and focusing upon sequencing and comprehension.

7. The final version is put into a book form, and illustrated by the children, and made part of the children's library for private reading, or for sharing with adults or peers or younger children.

Research :
It is reported by Laycock (1986) that such an exercise provides an opportunity to develop confidence and competence even among those children who have experienced difficulties and who have become reluctant to contribute, given their poor self-image as readers or writers.

Success in reading their own writing appears a major boost to the confidence of poor readers, according to the observations of a number of authors, notably Meek (1983).

References :
Laycock, E. (1986) Together we can do it.
Gnosis No. 8. ILEA. SPS.

Meek, M. (1983) Achieving Literacy.
London. Routledge and Kegan-Paul.

Activity : Paired Spelling (Parental Involvement)

Purpose : Enhancing accuracy and fluency of spelling via parental support.

Age Levels : Year 3/4 to Year 9 (approximately).

Benefits :
1. No limit to number of pupils who could receive support.

2. No specialist skills or interventions are required.

3. No costs are involved.

4. Procedure is simple.

5. Positive school-parent partnership is fostered as well as direct parental involvement with child's education.

6. Rapid progress may be achieved both in spelling and in self-confidence/motivation.

Strategy :
1. Spelling level is assessed and a "target" group of pupils is identified (e.g. by a criterion of a given percentage of spelling errors in a piece of free writing).

2. Target group given short dictation, and the errors are used to form the list of words to be learnt.

3. Each word selected is linked with four others according to word shape or letter string, rather than sound, e.g. heard - learn, earth, ear, pear.

4. Parent applies the "Look-Say-Cover-Write-Check" approach, following brief instruction at school (by class teacher, SEN Co-ordinator, or EP). Words are taught in groups of 5. Once learnt, the words are to be part of a written sentence dictated by the parent and, finally, written from memory.

5. Each group of 5 words is to be checked on 2 consecutive days by means of inclusion in a sentence and writing from memory.

6. Words from previous sessions are to be practised at random intervals.

Research :
Using a sample of pupils drawn from a mixed ability group in the intake year of a comprehensive school, Hewson (1990) reported marked improvements in spelling as measured by the change in the percentage of errors between initial and follow-up testing over a 5 week period (with 10 minutes a day set aside for the procedure). Further, pupil and parent reports referred to enthusiasm for the project, to self-confidence in the children, and to the rapid progress achieved by means of the specific procedure set down.

Reference :
Hewson, J. (1990) Paired Spelling.
Support for Learning. 5.3. 136-140.

(This article contains a model set of instructions; and one notes that the procedure could be applied by other adults, or older pupils.)

Activity : Paired Reading

Purpose : Increasing the accuracy and fluency of reading.

Age Levels : Year 3 to Year 7/8 (reading age approaching 7 year old level).

Benefits :
1. Simplicity of procedure and clear structure.

2. "Programme" can be implemented at home or at school with the help of teacher, parent, or any adult/older pupil.

3. Child has the experience of "Real Reading", and the emphasis is shifted away from errors/failure.

4. Procedure can be geared to the needs of the child, in terms of reading level, choice of reading matter, and pace.

5. Any number of children in a class may be assisted.

6. No specialist expertise is assumed.

Strategy :
1. Choose a book suitable for the child's age that s/he would like to read.

2. Select a quiet place where child and partner can sit side by side to see the book.

3. Child and partner begin by reading aloud together, with the pace to be slowed if the child falls behind. Partner may point to the words and if the child does not read a word, the partner points to it and encourages the child to try it again. The partner does not slow down or cease reading to see if the child can manage alone.

4. When the child signals (by tapping) to try reading alone, the partner stops reading, praises the child for signalling, allows the child to read alone and maintains a constant flow of praise/feedback while s/he reads correctly. If a mistake is made, the word is indicated and the child is encouraged to try again. The child is not asked to sound words out bit by bit.

5. If the child is stuck on a word for 4-5 seconds, the partner supplies the word and then they read the word together. Partner and child then continue reading together until the child signals again to read alone.

N.B. A daily session is required ideally for 15 minutes. Each session begins with reading together, and the child is allowed to change books as s/he wishes. Using a relatively difficult book is acceptable, and simply means reading together for a longer period.

Partner will talk about the content and pictures, and keep a record of progress to share with those others concerned with the child.

Research :
An initial project, involving parents of a group of reading retarded children, was set up by Morgan and Lyon (1978) in a primary school.

After a 6-month period, all the children had achieved marked progress, with a mean increase in accuracy of 11 + months and a similar increase in comprehension, according to the Neale Analysis.

Reference :
Morgan, R. and Lyon, E. (1979) Paired Reading: A preliminary report on a technique for parental tuition of reading retarded children.
Journal of Child Psychology & Psychiatry. 20. 151-160.

Further research demonstrating positive outcomes :
Robson, D. et. al. (1984) The Development of Paired Reading in High Peak and West Derbyshire.
Remedial Education. 19. 4.

Topping, K. (1987) Paired Reading Makes a Comeback.
Special Children Issue. 9. 14-15.

Activity : Peer Tutoring of Reading

Purpose : Enhancing Reading Accuracy Skills.

Age Levels : Primary Year 3 to Year 6/7

Benefits :
1. Relatively large numbers of pupils may be supported.

2. The programme is self-sufficient in the mainstream class involving no specialist intervention.

3. The programme may be easily accommodated in day to day routines, and may be implemented in short-time periods.

4. Gains are made by the more able as well as the less able readers.

5. No costs are incurred and no special material is required.

6. The programme is owned jointly by class teacher and children.

Strategy :
1. Class reading level is assessed using any (preferred) standard reading measure.

2. Class is divided into two groups ... the more able (hearers) and less able (readers).

3. Hearers and readers are paired, the most able hearer with the most able reader. Alternatively, if one targets, e.g. the 6 poorest readers, then such children will be paired with 6 hearers with whom they will be most compatible socially.

4. Time is set aside for sessions: e.g. a period of 30 minutes, twice a week.

5. Pairs are instructed as follows:
   (a) The reader begins each session by reading to the partner for at least 10 minutes.
   (b) When stuck, the reader is to look at the first letter, to look at the picture, to look at word shape, to read on and look back in context.
   (c) Words that are wrong, but which have the same meaning and maintain the sense of the story are allowed to stand and the reader is not interrupted.
   (d) Reader and hearer talk about the story and pictures.

Research :
Such a programme, established and evaluated by Leeves (1990), was found after one term to have brought about:-
   (i) Significant gains in reading accuracy in both readers and hearers.
   (ii) Enhanced enjoyment of reading, plus accurate selectivity of reading material based on greater awareness of reading competence.
   (iii) Greater insight into reading processes, i.e. the spelling of words, the significance of punctuation, etc.
   (iv) Enhanced general confidence and a feeling of control over learning processes.

Reference:
Leeves, I. (1990) Peer Tutoring.
Special Children. April 24.

Further Research Demonstrating Positive Outcomes.

Topping, K. (1988) The Peer Tutoring Handbook.
Educational Psychology 7. 2. 133-145

Limbrick, E. et. al. (1985) Reading gains for underachieving tutors and tutees in a cross age peer tutoring programme.
Journal of Child Psychology & Psychiatry. 26. 6. 939-553.

Observations and D.A.R.T.s materials

Appendix 4   D.A.R.T.s example

Pages 1 - 10

Observations and D.A.R.T.s materials
provided by a support teacher.

I became familiar with this class of children as a result of providing support for some pupils who had statements of Special Educational Needs. The negotiated support covered individual teaching and group activities to promote literacy skills, and group work relating to the class history topic. The teaching input took place in the Summer Term of Year 5.

Although the focus of all the teaching had to be for the statemented pupils, it soon became apparent that other children in my teaching groups also had poor literacy skills and showed similar symptoms of distractability and the same poor interpersonal skills as my statemented pupils. They were a very challenging and problematic teaching group. Discussion with the class teacher revealed that difficulties extended to many pupils within the class. Observation, when I was in the classroom showed groups of children who failed to stay on task and who interacted with each other inappropriately. Within my teaching groups, the dysfunctional nature of the children prevented them from concentrating on tasks even for a very short period of time and I felt that they had become disempowered to learn.

At the beginning of Year 6 I met with the class's new teacher to discuss the needs of the statemented pupils but I also discussed the broader needs of my group and the whole class as I had perceived them. Inevitably there were implications for classroom management in terms of developing the literacy skills of a large proportion of the class, helping them to function more appropriately socially and delivering the requirements of the National Curriculum. The class teacher and I explored together how the Directed Activities Related to Texts (D.A.R.T.s) might be useful in meeting many of the educational and social needs of the class. The class teacher was aware of D.A.R.T.s as a classroom strategy and we looked at ways of differentiating tasks within the activities.

The class constantly (one might say almost perpetually) challenged the working environment. Besides producing little work, they could not be trusted with equipment, however basic, and practical activities were really a non-starter. During the first six months of the academic year the class teacher was often in need of support to share the stresses and strains that this group generated. During this time, and indeed throughout the year, this was a role that I fulfilled. Despite the high level demands the class made, during discussions that the class teacher and I had, there were tangible signs of progress within the class.

At the end of the Spring Term, the teacher asked me if I could spare some time to come into the classroom in order to try and gauge how the class had progressed. At the time of my visit the class was undertaking a D.A.R.T. activity. On entering the classroom I was aware of a much lower level of noise and a sense of purposefulness amongst the class. Several pupils acknowledged me but did so quietly and then carried on working. The children were working in pairs and were obviously discussing the work together. All the groups in the room had equipment such as scissors and glue out and again these were being used appropriately. Two statemented pupils came to me and asked for help and then went away prepared to carry on working. Some children were around the class teacher, again wanting help. Those not being spoken to directly were waiting patiently and quietly sharing with each other where they needed help. This resolved difficulties for some of them. Not only was there a greater involvement with the learning process but the children came over as being happier in themselves and more responsive to the needs of those around them. At the end of the session the class left their work and equipment tidily on their desks and left the room in a quiet, orderly fashion.

It seemed that the combination of activities that the teacher had devised to raise self-esteem together with the consideration that had been given, appropriate curriculum access had significantly enhanced the children's ability to learn.

Margaret Byram

Directed Activities Related To Texts
D.A.R.T.s

This section is taken from "Practical Approaches to Differentiation; a handbook of ideas for teachers" by Margaret Byram, produced for The Service for Special Educational Needs, County of Avon.

For busy classroom teachers D.A.R.T.s provide curriculum focused learning support to each pupil in the class. They can be used across every curriculum area and their use can provide a multi-sensory approach to developing understanding for all age groups. The learning of all pupils is enhanced by using D.A.R.T.s; they are a means of providing enrichment and extension for pupils whatever their ability levels.

Their use in the classroom allows for:
1) Peer group support learning.
2) The use of texts at a higher level of readability.
3) A broad range of texts, both fiction and non-fiction, including poetry, journals, articles, charts.
4) A period of learning when all pupils interact on a task.
5) A variety of teaching and learning styles within any one activity.
6) Opportunities to observe pupils approaches to a task and identify barriers to learning.
7) Assessment of the pupil's ability to use higher order reading skills.

D.A.R.T.s is a term used to describe a range of classroom techniques that share one common feature; pupils are directed by the teacher to read a specified text in a particular way. The purpose of D.A.R.T.s is to promote active and reflective reading causing pupils to locate, process and present relevant information.

* A selected text should be worth reading/contain important information/be related to the curriculum

* Discussion during the activity is essential to clarify understanding. Pupils should work in pairs or in small groups.

D.A.R.T.s fall into two categories:-
    1. Reconstruction of text.
    2. Analysis of text.

1) Reconstruction of text includes:-
    a) Sequencing.
    b) Completion/Cloze.
    c) Prediction.

2) Analysis of text includes:-
    a) Underlining/locating information.
    b) Segmenting.
    c) Tabulation.

1a) Sequencing
Ordering of jumbled cut up text. Pupils need physically to move the pieces around.

e.g.. picture/sentence matching.
       putting sentences in the correct order.

sequencing paragraphs.
sequencing a mixture of phases, sentences and paragraphs.
sequencing words in a short poem.

Uses:
ordering the plot of a story.
ordering the events in a historical situation e.g. The Great Fire of London.
ordering the steps in a process e.g. making paper.
ordering instructions e.g. how to make a cup of tea.
recipes.

1b) Completion/Cloze

Pupils fill in teacher chosen deletions. These may be single words, phases or even whole sentences or verses. The value of the activity depends on the choice of deletions. These could be descriptive words, rhyming words or key content words in a topic-based passage. Labels on diagrams can also be deleted and the text used to decide what the missing labels are.

The section on Four Step Cloze Procedure provides fuller information about this activity.

1c) Prediction

Pupils construct the next stage of the text by referring to the given text. Group discussion to justify reasons is vital.

Uses: predicting the development of plot in fiction. This activity is more suited to fiction than information texts.

2a) Underlining/locating information
Pupils find and mark by underlining, highlighting or circling the information asked for by the teacher e.g., "Find the words which tell you what cavemen used to make their paint. Underline them in red." Discussion and feedback are essential for deciding on what is relevant and what is redundant information.

The D.A.R.T. activity included in this appendix uses this technique.

2b) Segmenting

Pupils identify and mark blocks of meaning. This activity is usually accompanied by labelling or summarising. This can be used to subdivide long paragraphs into smaller blocks of meaning or ideas. Labels in the margin summarise the ideas.

2c) Tabulation

This follows underlining as a means of representing the information located in the text. Lists, diagrams, flow charts or tables can be constructed or completed once the required information has been found in the text, e.g.

i) Underline and number the steps in the process of making paper. Draw a flow diagram to show the stages in the process.

ii) Underline in red the parts which tell us what fish are like. Underline in blue the parts which tell you what whales are like.

An example of a D.A.R.T., together with a set of Teachers' Notes is included in this appendix. If teachers and pupils are unused to the demands of D.A.R.T's, it is useful to follow the structure provided in the notes. With increasing confidence and skill, it will become possible to present the initial reading task to pupils in a variety of ways to meet their needs.

Example of D.A.R.T. Activity

Cortes' Expedition to Mexico
Designed by Chris Tippetts,
Manorbrook Juniors.
Additional material by Margaret Byram: Northavon SSEN.

A D.A.R.T. activity originally designed for a mixed class of Year 5 and 6 children with a wide range of ability levels.

The pack consists of:
- **A) Teachers' Notes.**
- **B) The Text.**
- **C) Outcomes:**
    - i) Sequencing and example of how to present to pupils
    - ii) Differentiated cloze passages
    - iii) Inferential writing
    - iv) Imaginative writing
    - v) Picture labelling

Outcomes iii) and iv) could be recorded using the other media e.g.
- tape recorder
- painting
- poster

Notes. Read through carefully before working with the pupils.

1. Pair an able reader with a less able reader for the directed reading activity.
2. The sequencing task followed by the appropriate level cloze activity are suggested by the first outcomes as a check that the text has been understood.
3. The other activities can follow in any order.

Instruction for Directed Reading Activity

1. Read the passage through to pupils twice.
2. All pupils and teacher read text together.
3. Underline in red all the things that Cortes heard about the Great Empire.
4. Underline in green all the things taken by Cortes on his trip to Mexico.
5. Underline in blue words and phrases that describe the journey to Tenochtitlan.
6. Underline in yellow words and phrases that tell you about the role of Cortes' men used in their fight against the Indians.
7. Underline in brown words and phrases that tell you about the role of Cortes in the diminishing Aztec civilisation.
8. Underline in pencil words and phrases that show you how the Indians accepted Cortes.

* Ensure that each pair of pupils has the appropriate crayons prior to starting the activity.

** Check the underlining at each stage before moving on. This ensures all pupils have information underlined and provides many opportunities for discussion.

How Did Cortes and His Men Conquer the Aztec Empire?

Hernan Cortes was ten years old when news reached his town in Spain that Christopher Columbus had crossed the great ocean sea. As Cortes grew up he heard stories of a great empire in the West, full of gold and jewels. He longed to go there. He went first to Cuba. There he worked hard and became rich and important. He owned farms and mines. He wanted more than anything to rule a land of his own. Then the governor of Cuba asked him to lead an expedition to the mainland. This was Cortes's great chance.

In 1519 Cortes sailed for Mexico. He took with him 11 ships and 100 sailors, 508 soldiers, 16 horses, a few cannons and some muskets. They all landed safely on a part of Mexico which had not been explored before. Cortes burnt all the ships which had brought them there. There was no going back.

Then Cortes ordered some of his men to stay behind. Cortes and 400 Spaniards began their long march to Tenochtitlan. They marched through steamy hot jungles. They marched over high mountains where the winds were icy. They fought off attacks by thousands of fierce Indian warriors. Cortes and his men always won. They used muskets, which the Indians had never seen before. The Indians were amazed. They began to believe that Cortes was a god. Different Indian tribes agreed to fight with Cortes against the Aztecs, whom they hated and feared. Meanwhile, in Tenochtitlan, Montezuma listened to what his spies told him. He watched and waited.

from "Exploration and Encounters"
This extract is reproduced by kind permission of Heinemann.

Sequencing Activity

Enlarge and photocopy for each child. Card covered with tacky back is more durable. Cut into strips; jumble prior to giving out. Put into envelopes, strips can be distributed and stored easily.

Cortes sailed to Mexico in 1519.	Cortes burnt all the ships.
Montezuma, the leader of the Aztecs, decided not to fight against the Spaniards.	
The governor of Cuba asked Cortes to invade Mexico.	
Cortes heard stories about Columbus when he was a young boy.	
Cortes led his men on a march to Tenochtitlan.	

Appendix 4 page 5

Example of Four Step Cloze Procedure

Stage 1

Cortes' Expedition to Mexico.

Read each sentence from beginning to end and say "mmmm" when you come to the space.

Choose a word from the box that will make the sentence make sense.

Read the whole sentence with the word you have chosen before you write it in.

strange	was	great
Cortes	lived	four hundred
lead	thought	difficult

1. Cortes wanted to find the ____ land he had heard so much about.

2. When he ____ in Cuba, he became very important.

3. He was asked to ____ an expedition to Mexico.

4. The expedition ____ very big.

5. Cortes and ____ of the men set off to march to the Aztecs' city.

6. They had a ____ journey.

7. They defeated the Indians by using ____ weapons.

8. The Indians ____ Cortes was a god.

9. They decided to help ____ fight the Aztecs.

Now read your work through carefully.

Ask someone to read it to you.

Does your work make sense?

Appendix 4 page 6

Example of Four Step Cloze Procedure

Stage 2

Cortes' Expedition to Mexico.

Read each sentence from beginning to end and say "mmmm" when you come to the space.

Think of a word that will make the sentence make sense.

Read the whole sentence with the word you have chosen before you write it in.

1. Cortes wanted to find the _____ land he had heard so much about.

2. When he _____ in Cuba, he became very important.

3. He was asked to _____ an expedition to Mexico.

4. The expedition _____ very big.

5. Cortes and _____ of the men set off to march to the Aztecs' city.

6. They had a _____ journey.

7. They defeated the Indians by using _____ weapons.

8. The Indians _____ Cortes was a god.

9. They decided to help _____ fight the Aztecs.

Now read your work through carefully.

Ask someone to read it to you.

Does your work make sense?

Example of Four Step Cloze Procedure

Stage 3

Cortes' Expedition to Mexico.

Read each sentence from beginning to end and say "mmmm" when you come to the space.

Think of a word that will make the sentence make sense.

Read the whole sentence with the word you have chosen before you write it in.

strange	was	great
Cortes	lived	four hundred
lead	thought	difficult

Cortes wanted to find the _____ land he had heard so much about. When he _____ in Cuba, he became very important. He was asked to _____ an expedition to Mexico. The expedition _____ very big. Cortes and _____ of the men set off to march to the Aztecs' city. They had a _____ journey. They defeated the Indians by using _____ weapons. The Indians _____ Cortes was a god. They decided to help _____ fight the Aztecs.

Now read your work through carefully.

Ask someone to read it to you.

Does your work make sense?

Example of Four Step Cloze Procedure

Stage 4

Cortes' Expedition to Mexico.

Read each sentence from beginning to end and say "mmmm" when you come to the space.

Think of a word that will make the sentence make sense.

Read the whole sentence with the word you have chosen before you write it in.

Cortes wanted to find the _____ land he had heard so much about. When he _____ in Cuba, he became very important. He was asked to _____ an expedition to Mexico. The expedition _____ very big. Cortes and _____ of the men set off to march to the Aztecs' City. They had a _____ journey. They defeated the Indians by using _____ weapons. The Indians _____ Cortes was a god. They decided to help _____ fight the Aztecs.

Now read your work through carefully.

Ask someone to read it to you.

Does your work make sense?

Label the picture carefully so that you show the differences between the Spanish invaders and the Aztecs.

Some labels are in place.

The text might help you with the spellings.

Colour the picture carefully. This may show the differences.

Appendix 4 page 9

This Aztec picture shows Cortes fighting

Cortes' Expedition to Mexico.

What do you think happened after the Indians decided to help Hernan Cortes?

_____
_____
_____
_____

Can you give some reasons why you thought this?

_____
_____
_____
_____

You are with Cortes marching to the Aztec City.

Write a short entry in your journal or a poem describing what it was like on the march and how you felt.

Bibliography

Appendix 5   Bibliography

Pages 1 - 4

Bibliography

Ainscow, M. (ed.) (1991) Effective Schools for All.
David Fulton, London.

Ainscow, M. and Florek, A.(ed.) (1989) Special Educational Needs: Towards a Whole School Approach.
David Fulton and National Council for Special Education.

Ainscow, M. and Tweddle, D. (1979) Preventing Classroom Failure: An Objectives Approach.
Chichester, Wiley and Sons.

Barton, L. and Landman, M. (1993) The Politics of Integration: Observations on the Warnock Report, Slee, R.(ed.)
Falmer Press.

Best, R. (1991) Support Teaching in a Comprehensive School. Some Reflections on Recent Experience.
Support for Learning. Vol. 6.(i) (1991)

Bliss, T. & Tetley, J. (1993) Circle Time.
Lame Duck Publishing, Bristol.

Brandes, D. & Phillips, H. (1977) The Gamester's Handbook.
Stanley Thornes, Cheltenham.

Brandes, D. (1982) The Gamester's Handbook Two.
Stanley Thornes, Cheltenham.

Byram, M. (1994) Practical Approaches to Differentiation.
Avon LEA.

Caldecott, L. Durbin, N. & Siner, J. (1993) Developing co-operation in The Primary School.
Cheshire County Council.

Canter, L. & Canter, M. (1976) Assertive Discipline.
Lee Canter Associates, Santa Monica.

Cooke, S.(1989) Keeping in Touch with Reality: the Role of a Special Needs Co-ordinator in a Secondary School, in Mel Ainscow (ed.) Special Education in Change.
London, Fulton and Cambridge Institute of Education.

Dept. for Education. (1995) English in the National Curruriculum.
London. HMSO.

Dept. of Education and Science. (1989) National Curriculum From Policy to Practice.
London, HMSO.

Dept. of Education and Science. (1990) Special Needs Issues, a Survey by HMI.
London, HMSO.

Dept. for Education.(1994) Code of Practice on the identification and assessment of special educational needs.
Central Office of Information. London.

Dewar, R., Palser, K. & Notley, M. (1989) Games, Games, Games.
The Woodcraft Folk, London.

Dyson, A. (1994) Effectiveness for All: Towards a Collaborative Learning Model for Responding to Student Diversity.
Support for Learning, Vol.9. No. 2.

Fox, G. (1988) A Handbook for Special Needs Assistants Working in Partnership with Teachers.
Fulton, London.

Gilbert, C. and Hart, M. (1990) Towards Integration.
London, Kogan Page.

Gordon, T. (1974) Teacher Effectiveness Training.
David McKay Co., New York.

Heseltine, P. (1987) Games for all Children.
Blackwell, Oxford.

Hopkins, D. (1985) Teacher's Guide to Classroom Research.
O.U. Milton Keynes.

Jeffs, A. (1991) Differentiation, Guidelines for Staff.
Service for Special Educational Needs, Avon.

Jenkins, D. & Jones, P. (1990) From Planning to Profile.
Language & Learning No.3 June 1990, pp 16-21.

Kilpatrick, A. & McCall, P. & Palmer, S. (1988) I See What You Mean. Vol. 1 & 2.
Oliver & Boyd.

King, V. (1990) Differentiation is the Key.
Language & Learning No.3, June 1990, pp 22-24.

Kitson, N. & Merry, R. (1992) Is it a bird, is it a plane...?.
Language and Learning No. 10, July 1992, pp 5-7.

Kyriacou, C. (1986) Effective Teaching in Schools.
Oxford, Blackwell.

Meynell . (1993) Parachute Play.
Maynell Games Publications, London.

Moon, B. (1990) New Curriculum - National Curriculum.
OU, Hodder and Stoughton.

National Curriculum Council. (1989) Curriculum Guidance, 1A, Framework for The Primary Curriculum.
York, N.C.C.

National Curriculum Council. (1989) Curriculum Guidance 2A, Curriculum for All: Special Educational Needs in the National Curriculum.
York, N.C.C.

National Curriculum Council. (1990) Curriculum Guidance 3, The Whole Curriculum.
York, N.C.C.

National Curriculum Council. (1989) Circular Number 5, Implementing the National Curriculum - Participation by Pupils with Special Educational Needs.
York, N.C.C.

National Curriculum Council. (1989) A Curriculum for All: Special Educational Needs in the National Curriculum.
York, NCC.

National Curriculum Council. (1991) Science and pupils with Special Educational Needs.
York, NCC.

National Curriculum Council. (1993) Teaching Science at Key Stage 1 & 2.
York, NCC.

NCET. (1994) The Portable Computer Pilot Evaluation Summary.

Norwich, B. (1990) Special Needs in Ordinary Schools.
Cassels, London.

OFSTED. (1993) Handbook for the Inspection of Schools.
London, HMSO.

Olsen, S. & Parker, J. (1988) Parachute Games.
Peace Pledge Union, London.

Pollard, A. and Tann, S. (1987) Reflective Teaching in the Primary School.
Cassell Education, London.

Postlethwaite, K. and Hackney, A. (1988) Organising a School's Response.
Basingstoke and London, Macmillan Education Ltd.

Pumphrey, P. and Reason, R.(1991) Specific Learning Difficulties (Dyslexia).
NFER/Nelson.

Raban, B. and Postlethwaite, K. (1988) Classroom Responses to Learning Difficulties.
Basingstoke and London, Macmillan Education Ltd.

Scher, A. & Verral, C. (1975) 100+ Ideas for Drama.
Heinemann Educational, London.

Spillman, J. (1991) Decoding Differentiation.
Special Children, No.44 January 1991, pp 7-10.

Stradling, R. and Saunders, L. with Weston, P. (1991) Differentiation in Action: A Whole School Approach for Raising Attainment.
National Federation for Educational Research, HMSO, London.

T.E.S. (1995) Much more than an extra pair of hands. 27.1.95.

Topping, K. (1988) The Peer Tutoring Handbook Promoting Co-operative Learning.
Croom Helm, London and Sydney.

Visser, J. (1993) Differentiation. Making it Work. Ideas for Staff Development.
NASEN, Stafford.

Visser, J. (1993) Special Education and Legislation: A Guide to the Education Act 1993 and OFSTED Inspections.
NASEN, Stafford

Visser, J. and Upton, G. (ed.) (1993) Special Education in Britain after Warnock.
David Fulton, London.

Warnock, M.(1978) Special Educational Needs: Report of the Commission of Enquiry into the Education of Handicapped Children and Young People.
HMSO.

Whittome, S. (1990) Classroom Organisation.
Language and Learning, No.3 June 1990, pp 3-8.

Wiltshire County Council. (1991) All Round Success.
Wiltshire County Council.

Don't forget to visit our website for all our latest publications, news and reviews.

www.luckyduck.co.uk

New publications every year on our specialist topics:

- **Emotional Literacy**
- **Self-esteem**
- **Bullying**
- **Positive Behaviour Management**
- **Circle Time**
- **Anger Management**
- **Asperger's Syndrome**
- **Eating Disorders**

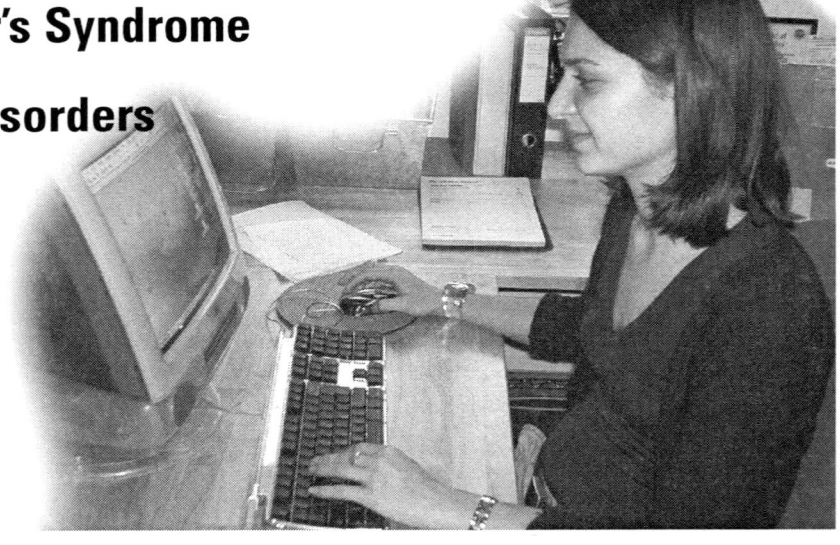

3 Thorndale Mews, Clifton, Bristol, BS8 2HX | Tel: +44 (0) 117 973 2881 Fax: +44 (0) 117 973 1707